Penguin Crossword Puzzle
Series Editor: Alan Cash

The Daily Telegraph
14th Crossword Puzzle Book

Clue: Beguiled? Bemused? Bored?

Answer: Hours of fun with the *Daily Telegraph* Crossword Books

Daily Telegraph Eighth Book of Crosswords
Daily Telegraph Ninth Book of Crosswords
Daily Telegraph Tenth Book of Crosswords
Daily Telegraph Eleventh Book of Crosswords
Daily Telegraph Twelfth Book of Crosswords
Daily Telegraph Thirteenth Book of Crosswords
Daily Telegraph Fifteenth Book of Crosswords
Daily Telegraph Sixteenth Book of Crosswords
Daily Telegraph 50th Anniversary Crosswords
Penguin Book of *Daily Telegraph* Quick Crosswords
Second *Daily Telegraph* Quick Crosswords

The Daily Telegraph
14th Crossword Puzzle Book

Penguin Books

PENGUIN BOOKS

Published by the Penguin Group
27 Wrights Lane, London W8 5TZ, England
Viking Penguin Inc., 40 West 23rd Street, New York, New York 10010, USA
Penguin Books Australia Ltd, Ringwood, Victoria, Australia
Penguin Books Canada Ltd, 2801 John Street, Markham, Ontario, Canada L3R 1B4
Penguin Books (NZ) Ltd, 182–190 Wairau Road, Auckland 10, New Zealand

Penguin Books Ltd, Registered Offices: Harmondsworth, Middlesex, England

First published in book form by Penguin Books 1978
10

Printed and bound in Great Britain by
Cox & Wyman Ltd, Reading
Set in Monotype Times

The Puzzles

1

Across

1 Youthful peasant who refuses to buy? (9)
8 The faint-hearted used to sniff at them (8-5)
11 Pale Aunt Sally? (4)
12 Cry of joy from someone who has little work (5)
13 Promising young bard (4)
16 A blade who would insultingly ignore a girl? (7)
17 Attempt to take in a queen to the hiding place (7)
18 He dispenses with specific ingredients (7)
20 Ruler of no charm originally (7)
21 Dead, but not dead on time (4)
22 Soft-headed, pert, priggish type (5)
23 To a degree the navy provides shelter (4)
26 It introduced point to the science of mathematics (7, 6)
27 Jack's party to celebrate the giant's downfall? (9)

2 Slow-moving birds (4)
3 Stereotyped phrases (7)
4 Got a tub designed for a 'tub' (7)
5 Test for the PM (4)
6 Arenas in which a politician has to warm Engineers in strikes (13)
7 He refuses to come out and whack the wrecker (6-7)
9 After the angler's haul about fifty fish get a chill (5, 4)
10 Toy prop? (9)
14 Bowl with the graduates batting (5)
15 Concerning ancient omission of Roman numerals (5)
19 Ground to soak up rain (7)
20 Somehow made use of venomous women (7)
24 Excellent alternative to time? (4)
25 What 20 down may have brushed as an afterthought (4)

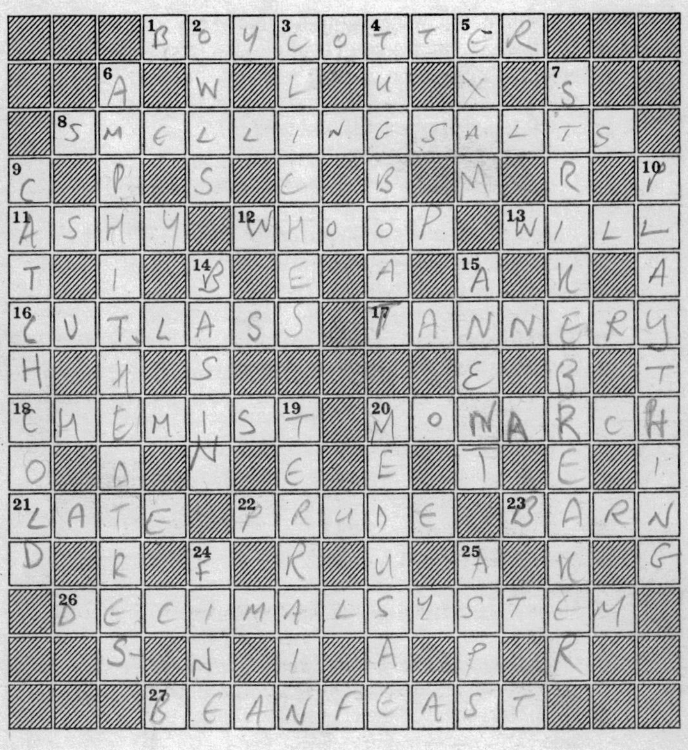

2

Across

1 Argumentatively the end of the line? (2, 3, 2, 2, 4)
10 Change nun made anon (7)
11 He may bribe to keep things working smoothly (7)
12 Idle bumpkin serving an apprenticeship? (4)
13 A tell-tale delivery at ground level (5)
14 Puts a stop to 3, maybe (4)
17 Get ready for the urn from arts master in Grecian territory (7)
18 Flustered sea bird coming from the Orient (7)
19 Late time for deliveries to start? (7)
22 Not one of two involved in three (7)
24 I, with the chemist, find them mischievous (4)
25 The fifth gang in Cheshire? (5)
26 A German who is equal to the count (4)
29 The amount of ground required by the Engineers in prison (7)
30 A transatlantic state or a Nazi organisation (7)
31 How the sleuth fails to keep Otto? (5, 3, 5)

Down

2 Exemplary worker occupying secure place in New Mexico (5, 2)
3 Objectives I put in a script (4)
4 An Italian poet making fairly slow progress to the bar (7)
5 Thankless critic of the church about to go over to the other side (7)
6 Works turns? (4)
7 The concentration required for driving on French motorways (7)
8 It generally means no work, though we can't bank on it (6, 7)
9 A man caught fighting (8, 2, 3)
15 Pull up on top of a lake in Italy (5)
16 Savoury Greek character in a Civil Service set-up (5)
20 Paper-making grass or paste mixture (7)
21 A pledge made by 18 (7)
22 Modern entrance for an old prison (7)

2

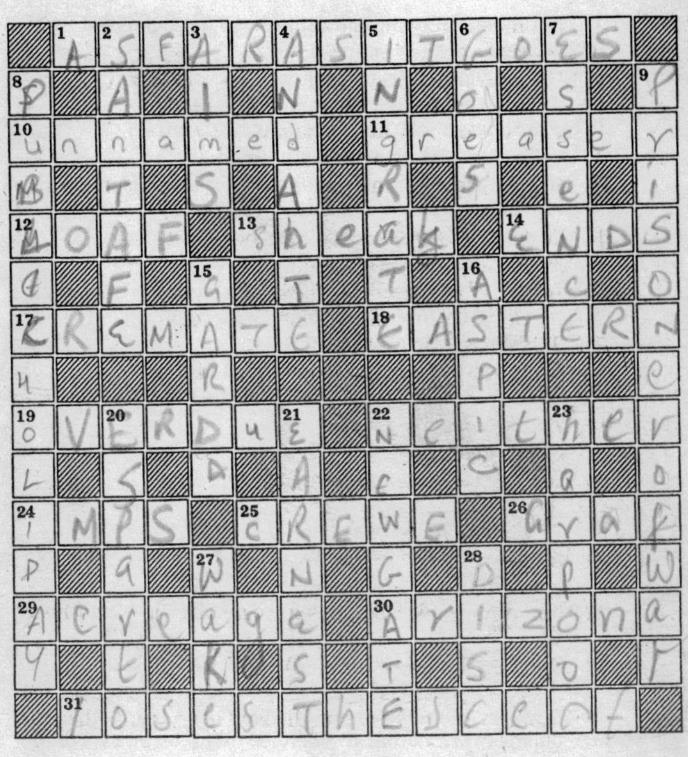

23 Keep talking about nothing but a killer of whales (7)
27 A festival looked back on in the main (4)
28 A record in which every word is clear (4)

3

Across

1 Teddy's family sounds appropriate to the Buffs (but isn't!) (8)
5 Saws for modern times? (6)
9 Writer to run away with the wife of Ulysses (8)
10 He prohibits a feature of the demonstration (6)
11 Drinks for game men on board (8)
12 Sliced lemons in seriously ceremonious form (6)
14 Previously used by another on watch? (6-4)
18 'Inspiring, bold John — ' (Burns: *Tam o'Shanter*) (10)
22 Neophyte without the means to grip (6)
23 Sinister direction of the radical worker (4-4)
24 Celestial circle that has ominous signs of the times (6)
25 Responsive, so be it talented (8)
26 Try air for a change of unusual value (6)
27 Attention given to Royalty in the big match (8)

Down

1 Upright walkers turn up 3.14159 in Bedfordshire (6)
2 An otherwise thin temper (6)
3 Algie's confused when pressed for fodder (6)
4 Intolerance of Gilbertian heroine claiming the opposite (10)
6 Hard-wearing suit for her best friend, reputedly (8)
7 Blue-grey scrap-iron? (3-5)
8 Evensong, alfresco and appassionato (8)
13 Qualified workman who should be useful on an expedition (10)
15 Nominally, Scrooge's chapel (8)
16 In favour of new drive for one who brings home the bacon (8)
17 Partiality for a swan-song? (8)
19 Immediately, or at some time in the past (2, 4)
20 Disorderly crowd's puddling-iron (6)
21 Refer to brief public announcement (6)

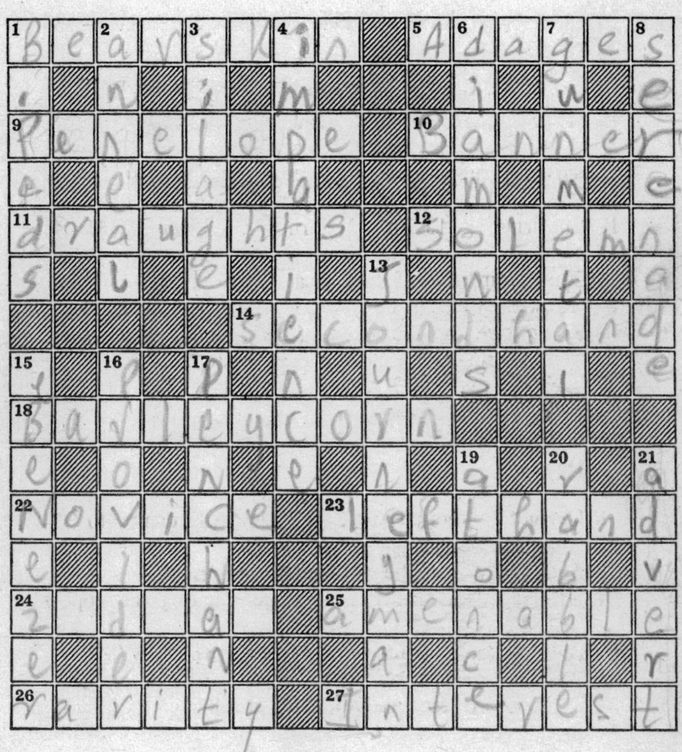

4

Across

1 and 9 What the fussy lyricist did, once he'd decided on his theme? (4, 1, 4, 5, 2)
10 A pig of a gale! (7)
11 The skill with which a Japanese folds his paper (7)
12 Refurbished gold tiara for old pro in the circus (9)
14 Intended to put things right again (8)
15 Bad storm coming to nothing on the coast of Norway (6)
17 A different throne? Or same again? (7)
20 Quakers among the woods (6)
23 The man called in to make a film for Mussolini, right? (8)
25 Positively taking a lengthy rest (5, 4)
26 Convert sea into land on the Baltic (7)
27 Latin composition on a cannibalistic insect (3-4)
28 Are called inside to put things in order (7)
29 Non-conformist Norfolk town I make an impression on (9)

Down

2 Like a ring of gunners coming up to abolish first (7)
3 What I need to make me a lord? (7)
4 She hurried round to a stylish furniture-maker (8)
5 Perplexed Gael holding foreign gold in abundance (6)
6 Acts the tyrant over those who perform round the pit? (9)
7 Somehow retains the bulk of the fat (7)
8 Irreproachable counsel to the overworked dyer! (9)
13 Small chapel to which Antony resorted after Caesar's death (7)
15 Once the accepted way for a Westminster man to get through to Fleet Street (6, 3)
16 Gloomy natures in confusion (9)
18 Returns from work? (8)
19 Clerks who send off bills, maybe (7)
21 Didn't get into deep water, but went canoeing, perhaps (7)
22 Old doctor off duty once a month? (3, 4)
24 Very pleased to make hay after knocking beer back! (6)

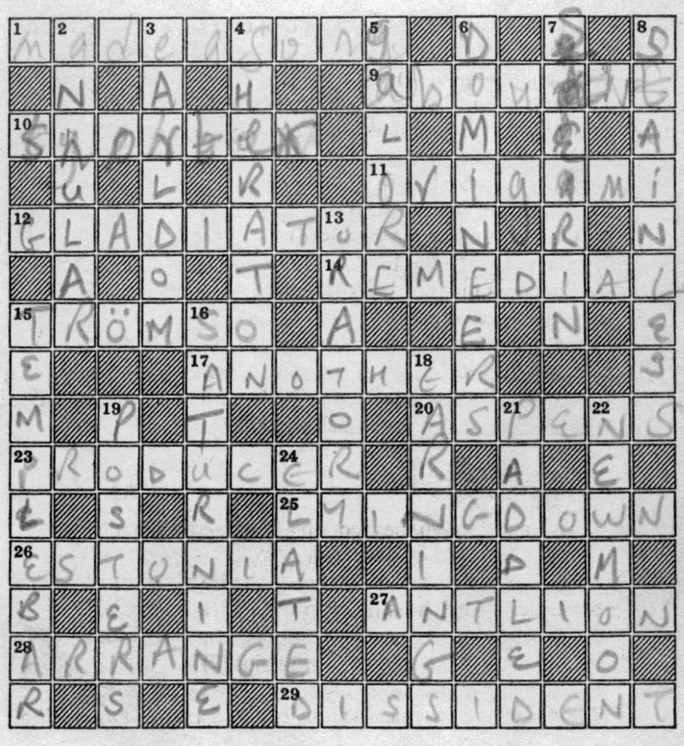

5

Across

7 Lacking social position, despite that (15)
8 Maybe the era of contraception and robbery (7)
10 Rescue in return for being abused (7)
11 Keen enough to agree to differ (5)
12 From French, German and English county (5)
14 Accidental sharp could be played on them (5)
15 We take the street opposite Number 9 (4)
16 Work till 1.50 (4)
17 No way to stalk – stalk by the river, that is (4)
19 Skin area (4)
21 The outcome of striking matches? (5)
22 Nose, spelt -o-e? (5)
23 Frequent description of what ghosts do (5)
25 Help an incarcerated friend, but leave in mid-air? (4, 3)
26 Attempts to reach Lawrence initially on the Adriatic (7)
27 Adoption of a current consumer policy? (15)

Down

1 Work up parasites to study steady Bobby (6-9)
2 Flapper to take a little food or drink (7)
3 Platform gates smashed (5)
4 Loafer indicates street sought by Holmes enthusiast (5)
5 Leading combatant of terrorist organisation in AD 1050 (7)
6 Presumably something is being made, but not enough of it (5-10)
9 The origin of teas? (4)
10 All the others do nothing (4)
13 One may be intoxicated by it, for example, during sunrise (5)
14 From behind see the old farm servants (5)
17 What polished thinkers do? (7)
18 No cold form of hate (4)
19 Meet a famous mountaineer (4)
20 Temporary accommodation in the ENE requiring international agreement (7)
23 Those in it probably cut dashing figures (5)
24 A path to follow (5)

6

Across

1 Procedural plan of the Metrication Board? (9)
9 Enter society with an invitation to play (4, 3)
10 Aircraft observer who developed the art of lifemanship (7)
11 Carry back the pitcher he painted (7)
12 Somehow ten famish – and collier goes down through it, too (4-5)
14 Left office but stayed another season? (8)
15 Learner fools the girls (6)
17 Try to be removed from that temptation (7)
20 Foot's old, old story (6)
23 Betting a science-fiction weapon may be used by those who would avoid a brush (5-3)
25 It measures miles by the feet (9)
26 Not one nor the other therein derived (7)
27 Minutely describes docks (7)
28 States unit in camera setting (7)
29 Unusual bear rates as one, of course (4, 5)

Down

2 Copy design of ear-clip (7)
3 Fish cleaners waste courses (7)
4 Yet maths produce something of value (8)
5 Card game to follow up to a point (6)
6 I am to act as a go-between without delay (9)
7 Monumental features written by journalists (7)
8 Lifeless as a fossil? (5-4)
13 To perform a single act of clemency is a give-away (4, 3)
15 Maybe it is not recognised by the High Church (3, 6)
16 Furniture the carpenter leaves to his apprentice? (4-5)
18 North East supports revision of police age far too old for us! (8)
19 Quietly brought up – but clearly not in a critical way (7)
21 Handy bomb? (7)
22 They have their points despite the blindness of their eyes (7)
24 Commotion caused by a lion rampant? (6)

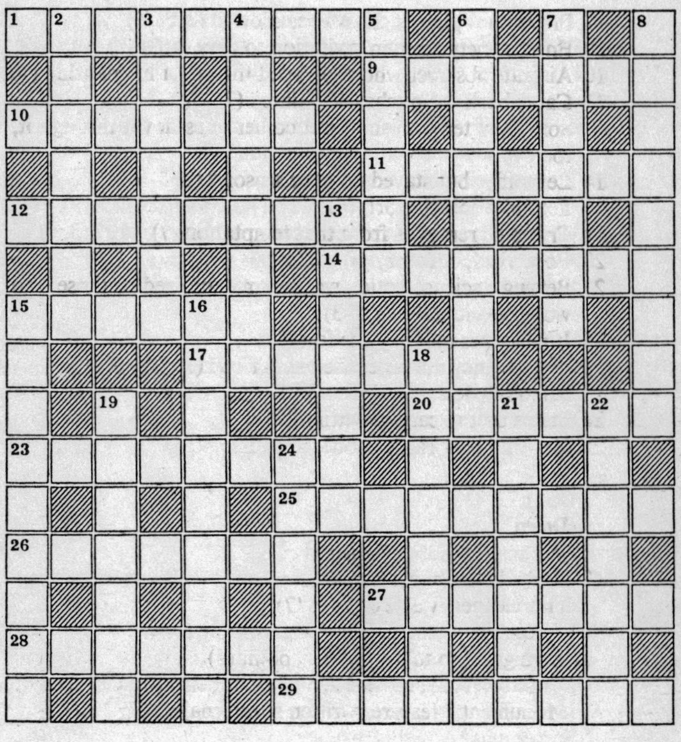

7

Across

1 Things that are bound to be borrowed (7, 5)
8 Old Norse threesome going round a lake in North America (7)
9 A fever centre I reorganised (7)
11 Cold 12 of unknown profundity in the main (7)
12 Fishing boat that sails with the tide? (7)
13 Diverting combinations of reel and line (2-3)
14 Not what the diner expects when he asks for sauce (9)
16 The only bit of time a busy eccentric has to spare? (3, 6)
19 A regressive attitude for a fabulous person (5)
21 Embankment of great antiquity evidently the worse for wear (7)
23 A mercenary of coarse fibre (7)
24 Pink country mansion surrounded by deer (7)
25 Take the place of one who is 18, maybe (7)
26 Special attire for the match (7-5)

Down

1 Pure maid holding the supply (7)
2 They use strong language, but draw the line at horses, apparently! (7)
3 Up against a team of six-footers? (9)
4 Submit a return (5)
5 Dismissed with a misplaced dive, lost the struggle? (7)
6 Upset tinker grasping a horny substance (7)
7 Someone who has taken cover having a plan of action? (6-6)
10 Wrote and agreed (12)
15 Make a snooker shot that is singularly effective (3, 3, 3)
17 The estate needs me to sort it out (7)
18 In a position to challenge all comers? (2, 5)
19 Sailor's love oddly free from blame (7)
20 The apiarist on board appears to be suffering from ague (7)
22 Subscription already paid or expected at any moment (3, 2)

7

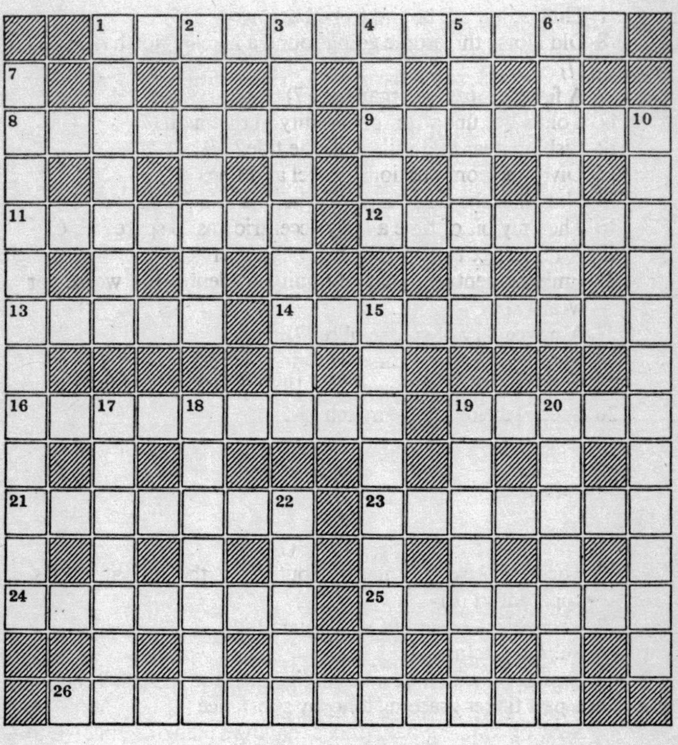

8

Across

1 Is he lighter than a flyweight? (6-5)
9 Young swimmer of Queen Catherine's family (4)
10 One who leaves his car in a curious position? (5, 6)
11 She loved Narcissus, it is recalled (4)
14 Speaking about the no-VAT category? (7)
16 Throw up a trophy? Must be drunk! (7)
17 First person to be present in spirit is an urchin (5)
18 Small number against a star (4)
19 Briefly not knowing a kind of cheese (4)
20 Shovels back the rest of nature (5)
22 Anything in New York is rather wicked (7)
23 Quarter to liaise somehow in Eastern Europe (7)
24 'Tell it not in —, publish it not in the streets of Askelon' (*Samuel* 2) (4)
28 Showgirl who might have shattered a Yankee lion (5, 6)
29 Craft in which one in France takes outside exercise (4)
30 He, silent, saw building of great fortune (11)

Down

2 Half hope of extreme case (4)
3 Acts for animals (4)
4 Sounds a thumping great area of London (7)
5 What we possess turns sour (4)
6 Butler's territory nowhere to be found (7)
7 How's that for a slogan? (5-6)
8 What a police-officer keeps up his sleeve (3, 2, 3, 3)
12 An abundance of evidence of footslogging in the Middle East! (4, 2, 5)
13 Jumpy enthusiast often seen in church (3, 8)
15 Was *The Beggar's Opera* written so light-heartedly? (5)
16 Records ten centuries in draws (5)
20 Remarkable scope a good man initiates (7)
21 Stewed rib chop, all piping (7)
25 Laid up, prone! (4)
26 Strip of hide (4)
27 Cat-calling gulls? (4)

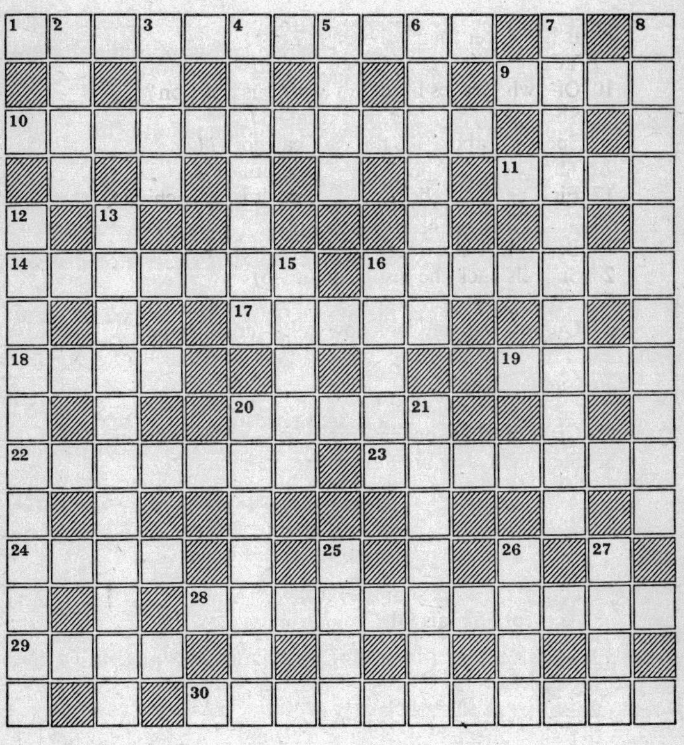

9

Across

1 Haloes for late motorists? (10)
8 Nothing daunted, the Spenserian lady went to the altar (6)
9 Enjoying a round of course? (2, 3, 5)
10 Man of practice taken in by a new boy (6)
11 Not returning after being on the job up North (10)
12 How many gained from distinction in etymology? (6)
13 A melody echoed in song (4)
15 Terse piece of writing about a pet dog (7)
19 Salad plant that may be taken with coffee (7)
21 'After the scole of Stratford — Bowe' (Chaucer: *Canterbury Tales*) (4)
22 Merry member of the March family with a small bottle of medicine (6)
25 A buck that's impressed? (6, 4)
27 The inane embodiment of classical wisdom (6)
28 Feature of a car that is used retrospectively (4, 6)
29 After-dinner drink I place before a Shakespearian heroine (6)
30 Sort of glider that one does not expect the plodder to have! (5, 5)

Down

1 Suitable bait for an angler making a complaint in the tropics? (4-4)
2 For them all work is play (6)
3 False statement on a large scale did much for chemistry (6)
4 The condition of the course on the way out? (5)
5 Girl enjoining silence about American Indian money (8)
6 Scornful Mediterranean islander with bent coin (8)
7 What happens in the German Dutch town (8)
13 Back at sea (3)
14 Woe betide the Arctic explorer that is caught therein! (3)
16 A minor take-over in the field of social welfare, maybe (8)
17 Large fish-forks (8)
18 Tree in flower in Cornwall is only a trifle (8)
20 Jaundiced with age? (8)
23 'Tis in craft he excels (6)

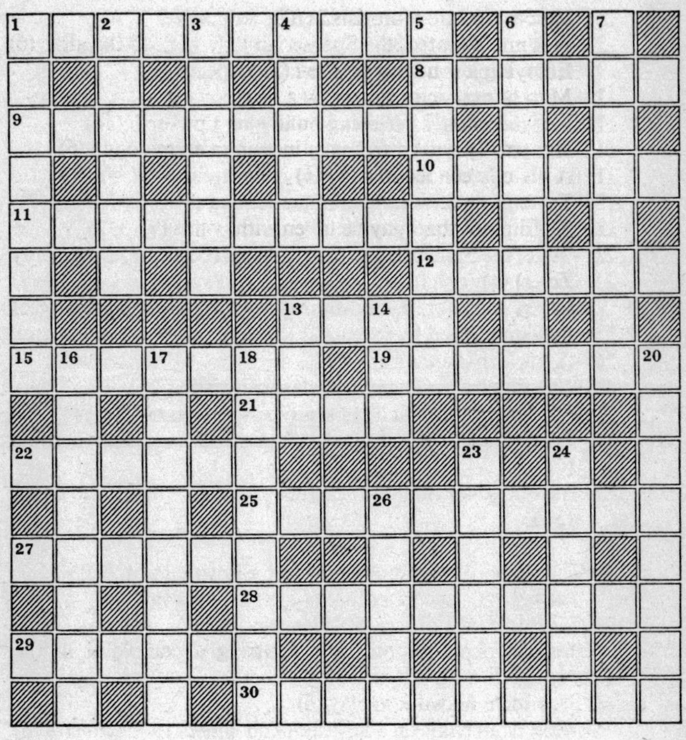

24 A fraud on which notes may be made (6)
26 Drunken churl, or his manner of progress, maybe (6)

10

Across

1 Not the kind that 'marches on its stomach'? (8, 4)
8 Faint graduate (4, 3)
9 Italian banker has need of East Europeans (7)
12 Hare changes into ostrich (4)
13 One who greatly admires 50 and over (5)
14 Back up the local member as an aid to inflation (4)
17 Briefly where a current failure may originate (2, 5)
18 Point to a dam which is enough to take one's breath away (7)
19 The liftman's query is the salesman's warning (5, 2)
22 Withdraw from the race as a response to irritation (7)
24 Did the mere sight of it make St David's enemies keel over? (4)
25 Lady unaffected by reversals (5)
26 Rail return cheat (4)
29 His fashionable manners irritate a worker (7)
31 Picture three famous Easterners entering in the East (7)
32 Two dreams in one suggest a degree of intoxication (6, 6)

Down

1 They cannot be only children on the hospital staff (7)
2 The first thirteen letters are of little matter (4)
3 Tried to move to part of Michigan (7)
4 Suffering from insomnia because utterly bereft of a pile? (7)
5 Fit and competent (4)
6 Beast from Malaya, Kurdistan and Tibet (3)
7 To a point parking's a stopper of this engine component (8-4)
10 Inarticulate but forcible expression (5)
11 First-rate warhorse for increasing the power output (12)
15 To express disgust for a ruffian (5)
16 Directors normally joined by a carpenter (5)
20 Cardsharp's suggestion which cannot be bettered (5)
21 Pie containing minced rats is valued in Turkey (7)
22 His wail is misconstrued as speech in parts of Africa (7)
23 Intuition, but not in teaching (7)
27 Mary, and what she had – as a surname (4)

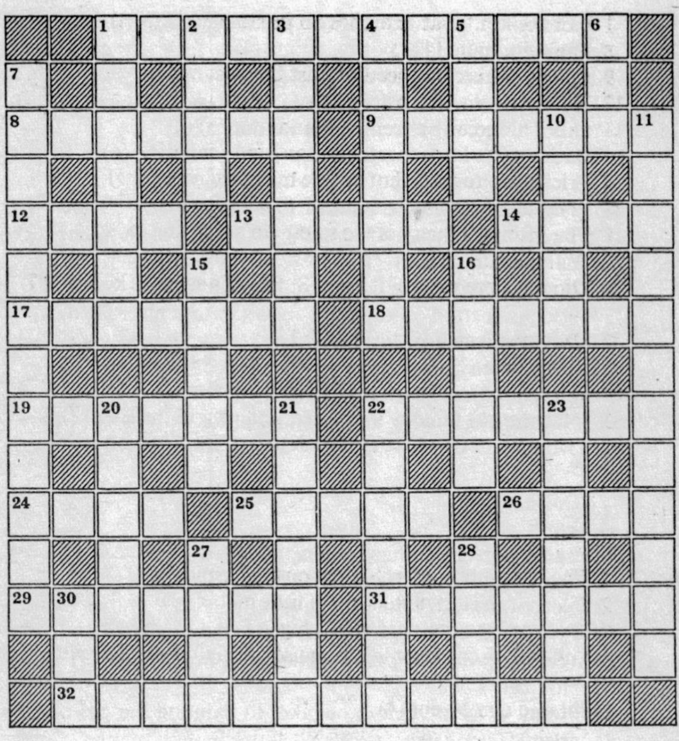

28 Bail out near Java (4)
30 In theological debate he may be needed to sum up (3)

11

Across

1 The hold that was doubly needed at Trafalgar (4-6)
6 Broken laws make boring points (4)
10 This bird is certainly no dodo (5)
11 Perhaps he comes from Cracow, or the end of the earth (5, 4)
12 Fool a doctor by turning lice in, that is (8)
13 Obviously not heavy land (5)
15 Draining the blood of a tenant? (7)
17 The cause of many a painful admission? (7)
19 Two graduates pass around the hat for an Asian teacher (7)
21 Fabulous horseman (7)
22 It rises in Africa and disturbs the reign (5)
24 Reconstruction of lead door for a treasure place (2, 6)
27 It is used extensively as an aid to far-sightedness (9)
28 Dwarf men go wild (5)
29 The fool fools become addicted to? (4)
30 Not the old Sunday School stand-in for daily sales (4-6)

Down

1 Lame word of military command (4)
2 6-0, 6-0, 6-0, engagement? (4, 5)
3 Never rattled? Not if you have it (5)
4 Permanent cause of irritation under the French (7)
5 Work socially acceptable advanced as worth a lot (7)
7 Not 25 (5)
8 Points to tee-up before he takes to painting the girl of his dreams (10)
9 Those of Israel were presumably a minority race (8)
14 Extremely happy about one half-minute out (10)
16 The aspect of investment that dispels boredom (8)
18 Switch positions, however vicissitudinous (2, 3, 4)
20 Bloomer caused by a couple of directions on the M1 (7)
21 Touching fellows who hawk (7)
23 Dance pronounced as appropriate for the Hunt Ball? (5)
25 Not left any entitlement (5)
26 Islands that present possibilities of opening up? (4)

11

12

Across

1 and 5 An illuminated address? (7, 7)
9 Apt description of what the Jumbo Jet marked in aeronautical design (4, 11)
10 Charon's modest fee (4)
11 A non-runner, naturally (5)
12 Owing to the left, it's now forbidden (4)
15 Sign one expects to see outside an exclusive establishment (4, 3)
16 Ferocious beast I'll go to the Royal Academy about (7)
17 They kept cool in the days of the Raj (7)
19 A piece of land or what may bring it into cultivation (7)
21 Disreputable solicitor 100 per cent. Gallic? (4)
22 Maybe curvaceous rebel against conventional morality (5)
23 Big plug for the liquor trade (4)
26 A very close contest (4-2-4, 5)
27 Information I'd preserve about the General Staff (7)
28 Piece of mosaic Mars put back (7)

Down

1 American tree on which there's no dead wood? (4-3)
2 We do all we possibly can to leave it (2, 5, 8)
3 Genial essayist revealing himself a little put out in retrospect (4)
4 Snuffs the candle and nimbly vacates the room? (4, 3)
5 Ocean swimmer about to ring up for sacking (7)
6 The key feature of a cycle factory (4)
7 Odd battle between ill-matched adversaries (7, 8)
8 One girl set at variance with another (7)
13 Fight about nothing but a raid (5)
14 Big US gun the Engineers brought in (5)
17 Casual attempt to pocket a ball? (3-4)
18 Hemmed in by mountain folk he sounds punitive (7)
19 Superior bow tie that won first prize? (3-4)
20 A wet race-meeting (7)
24 Cause bewilderment by striking (4)
25 They swim a foot between two points (4)

12

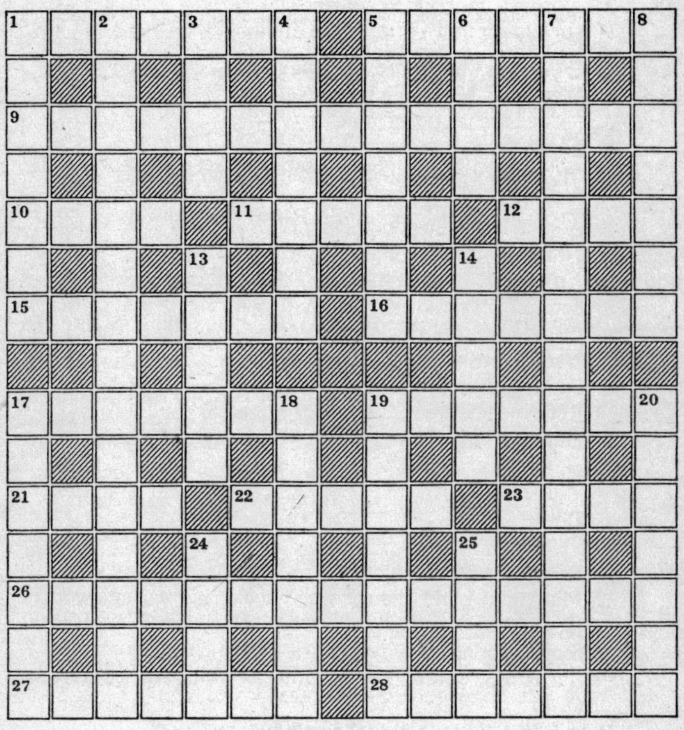

13

Across

1 and 5 Legal agreement to span the gap may be won by a trick (8, 6)
9 William is able to provide a camper's kettle (5-3)
10 Scratched, but won a point? (6)
12 Set right when covered again (9)
13 Niger diverted to royal ruling (5)
14 Morecambe entertainer booked little by little (4)
16 Pebbles on the roof (7)
19 A comparatively good helper (7)
21 Nominally she is a gaol-breaker (4)
24 An address in poetry for a positive Pole (5)
25 Set up tents beside a river where bell-ringing is at its height (9)
27 Natural hostelry at East end (6)
28 Shining above a South-coast resort (8)
29 Reformed desire to have one's home (6)
30 Hill poem transcribed for the poet's nightingale (8)

Down

1 Bavarian town for loafers? (6)
2 Making any old change won't make her a gentlewoman (2, 4)
3 Similar sound used by the lyric writer (5)
4 and 20 E.g. the Thousand Guineas or the Ancient Greeks (7, 4)
6 and 26 Celestial top of the note-makers? (9, 5)
7 Grace's or Wendy's folk, the dears! (8)
8 Conclusion to infuriate is put in jeopardy (8)
11 and 21 down If charm does become upset, Caesar was warned against it (4, 2, 5)
15 Stood another round and retired (9)
17 Supercilious opponent of Cromwell . . . (8)
18 . . . tells the tale of foreign noblemen (8)
20 See 4
21 See 11
22 As the injured party it turns up between six hundred and 1,000 (6)

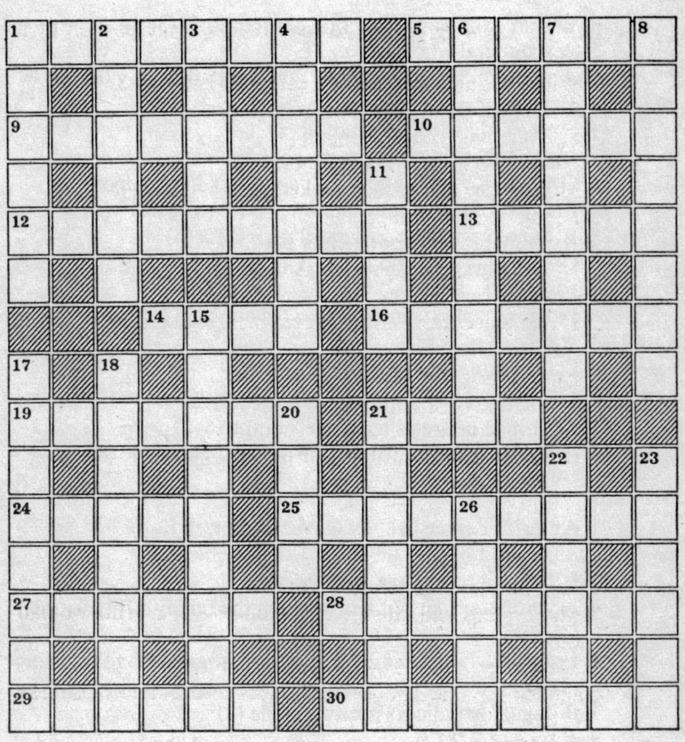

23 Barker's home (6)
26 See 6

14

Across

1 Left in conflict with morality, apparently (3, 5)
5 A scoundrel who foxes us? (3, 3)
9 An old foreign penitentiary that has had its day (8)
10 I'm not one to weaken (6)
11 State-recognised linesman (8)
12 Unusually firm on grass, maybe! (6)
14 Gradual loss that weakens a country's intelligence (5, 5)
18 Make further overtures about a very quiet fish? (10)
22 A dance garment no one will wear long (6)
23 Concerning the land of the Taj Mahal city I went quickly round (8)
24 No good telling him what makes one old! (6)
25 A school ruler? (8)
26 Stayed inordinately sober (6)
27 Extremely pleasant miniature railway in Venice (4, 4)

Down

1 An extra degree held by Oliver Cromwell (2-4)
2 Sit up and beg for an ersatz handkerchief (6)
3 Is holding rebel flags, possibly (6)
4 A youngster like William defining the Spanish Inquisition? (4, 6)
6 French daily containing a refreshing suggestion for a picnic (8)
7 Bilingual Middle East travel guide (8)
8 A type of 7 (8)
13 Pretty small group of swish producers? (5, 5)
15 Kind of cake swallowed by judges chosen to represent the Roman people (8)
16 Odd place in which oil turns up for one of the Muses (8)
17 The toboggan going round the pleasure-ground gave a scintillating display (8)
19 Mimic draped in New York linen (6)
20 The last of the 15, according to Bulwer Lytton (6)
21 Bound to be charged for? (6)

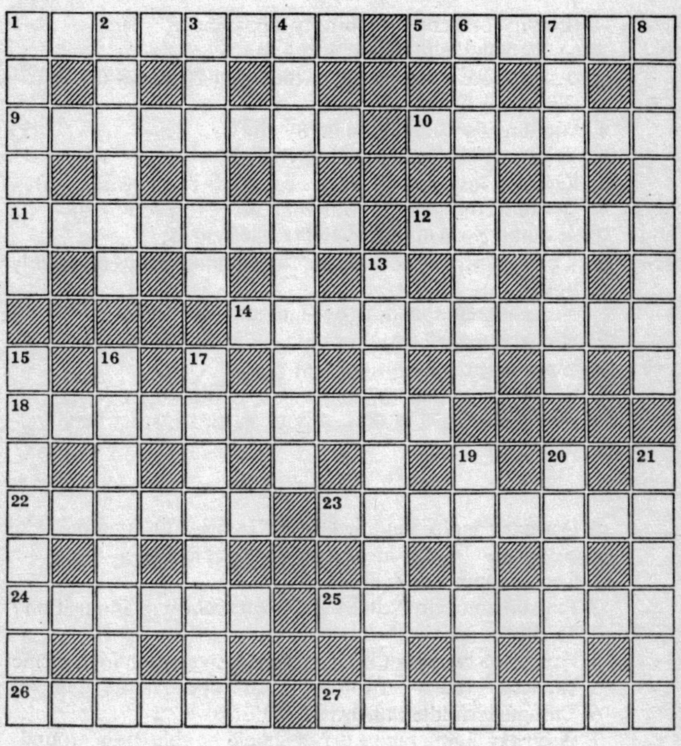

15

Across

1 Easter or Whitsun picnic? (7, 5)
8 Century old political division (7)
9 A vigorous blow in the passage (or a light tap) could extinguish it (3-4)
11 Beating drums to flatten the pitch? (7)
12 Vehicle-horse that goes pelting in Canada (7)
13 Part of a church anthem (5)
14 L-shaped fish-press (5-4)
16 A memory-jog about whatever is left (9)
19 Before or after distributing coal a trainee might make for it! (5)
21 Never scored, therefore not famous (7)
23 Sing about a gee-gee drooping at the middle (7)
24 White spirit, perhaps, but not so stout (7)
25 Bonus I'm arranging for use of travellers (7)
26 Put in a grave and pressed into shape to be set here and there (12)

Down

1 Chap in poor health needs a paper (7)
2 Finding an opera writer with half a cent (7)
3 Shield and defender (9)
4 Four twos in a row (5)
5 Take away freedom from an East European in the ENE (7)
6 Dash pole over a tent-dweller (7)
7 Electrical fault a racing driver should be able to get around quickly (5-7)
10 Head reader (12)
15 A revolutionary device for finding one's bearings (9)
17 Somewhat large accommodation for adult with child about one (7)
18 In grammar time is highly emotional (7)
19 Stories of some feet? (7)
20 Pilfered a couple of resting-places (7)
22 Precious violin turned up to be played in 19 across, maybe (5)

15

16

Across

1 A fault not long showing up (11)
8 Suggestion which supports the situation (11)
11 Meal prepared for a manly type (4)
12 He ruled with the heart of a sinner once (4)
12 Don't drink? Tars ain't changed! (7)
15 Were any resolving when it arrived? (3, 4)
16 Imbibes much from top quarters (5)
17 She had a rough house (4)
18 Where non-European material is turned into articles (4)
19 Postpone or submit? (5)
21 Their practice is to give patient attention (7)
22 Wind instrument includes song transmitted through another station (7)
23 File eighteenth letter like the sixteenth (4)
26 Those who keep watch should have it, if not too busy (4)
27 A rule which is flexible (4-7)
28 Currently operated against the advice of the ironing-machine handbook? 5-6)

Down

2 Pronouncedly higher rent (4)
3 Model person altered it to store (7)
4 The price of a lettuce exactly? (4)
5 Words of wisdom to keep Tom up on his toes (7)
6 All off at the end of the morning (4)
7 Somehow boards amass top representatives (11)
8 Daub the actors to make an impression (7, 4)
9 Persevere in the invariable use of euphemisms to indicate death (5, 3, 3)
10 Their turns are essentially concerned with exits and entrances (4-7)
14 Money for a song? (5)
15 Points a parson backs not at all (5)
19 Debtors about finished, but they still take stock (7)
20 I strive to reform, but go back again (7)
24 Two of equal value I included (4)
25 He has Rifle Brigade support for a season (4)

16

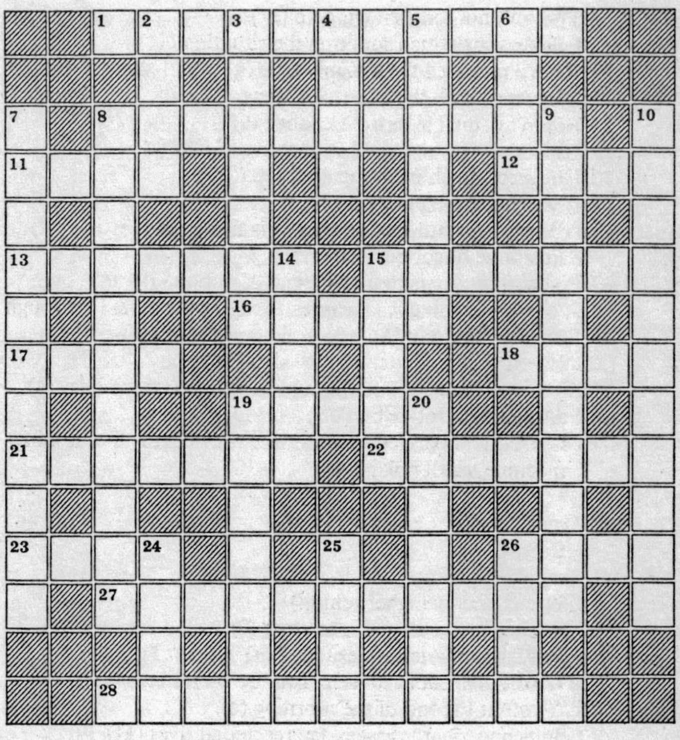

26 24 + one (4)

17

Across

1 The wisdom with which the doe regards what has happened? (9)
8 Final check by a knight explaining what Othello did (9, 4)
11 The wet season artist in the South (5)
12 Bones of equal length that meet in the middle? (5)
13 Express a view about a musical work in E (5)
16 Isolated Greek nectar product (6)
17 If you can't, that's best? Get away with you! (4, 2)
18 A Muse expressing hesitation at nothing (5)
19 Sailor investing money in riotous festivity (6)
20 Points to average kind of lion slain by Hercules (6)
21 A confederate outwardly calm (5)
24 Minister who lost American colonies, but won the Civil War (5)
26 Basic earnings we'd all like to see reduced! (5)
27 Still fighting? (6, 7)
28 Maybe frowns over the day's news (9)

Down

2 Trivial little things, one to turn as finishing (5)
3 Stopped and prepared a plan? (4, 2)
4 Maybe a skater who is extra busy during a heat wave (6)
5 Norwegian town in which a market is held (5)
6 It can double the effectiveness of the manual worker (13)
7 Go in for astrology, as film critics do? (5, 3, 5)
9 Contriving to get non-amateur remedial treatment (9)
10 Frolicsome friends X is put among (9)
13 Russian lake of no age (5)
14 Totally unfit for work outside North America (2, 3)
15 Black wood (5)
22 Twisted candle given surgical treatment (6)
23 Base from which we walk a little way (6)
25 Small railway terminus in Kent (5)
26 Plunder to which a soldier is entitled (5)

17

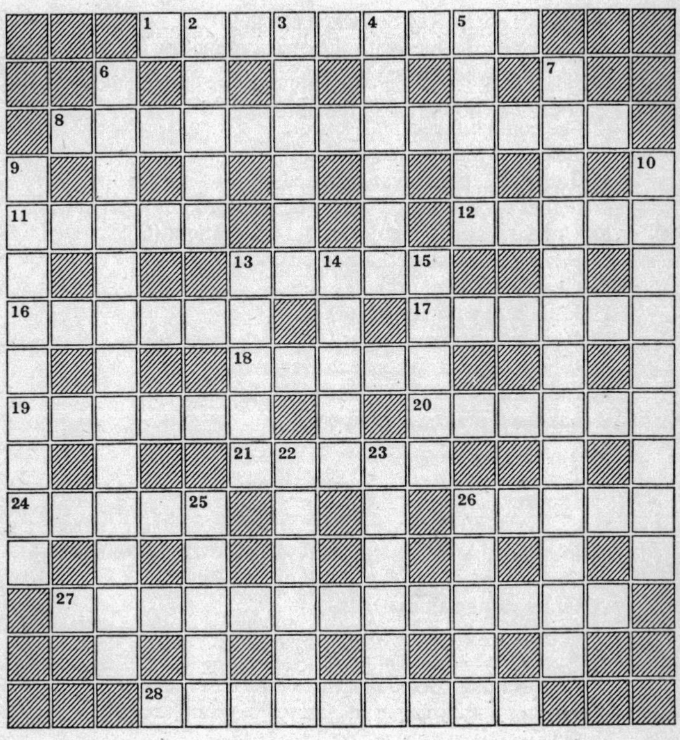

18

Across

1 Colour of the Red Sea when rough (6)
4 Showing off a bird with the object of mating (8)
9 Ill-fed maybe, but satisfied (6)
10 One who follows a good lead? (8)
12 She could be cruel with less (4)
13 Bales out with sophistication (5)
14 Tail of a 3, pointed and lopped (4)
17 Settles for leading parliamentarians (5, 7)
20 Upheaval Scots' ain rule could bring about (6, 6)
23 Favour that's something to be thankful for (4)
24 Gem of a wicket? (5)
25 Find fault with the fish (4)
28 How to beat the streaker? (8)
29 Where one's at variance in Devon (6)
30 Indolent to the very marrow? (4, 4)
31 Exclusive seat on a Jumbo (6)

Down

1 Disreputable lot among the Red Shadow's following? (4-4)
2 The answer to a sticky question, possibly (8)
3 Grass-raising animals (4)
5 It's why I claim it might be a fanciful characteristic (12)
6 Apprehend a familiar name (4)
7 Effect of one elected member on part of the play (6)
8 Get hot and bothered in a minority group area (6)
11 One you have to be awake to take (8-4)
15 Drinks up to get sharp (5)
16 A blooming forgery of £25 note! (5)
18 Indeed hot all went (8)
19 Standing by a working pickpocket, in case of necessity (2, 1, 5)
21 Take in with the eye of a sailor (6)
22 Place of low tension in 23 (6)
26 Case of the French in the Tuileries (4)
27 Did Leander give her a ring? (4)

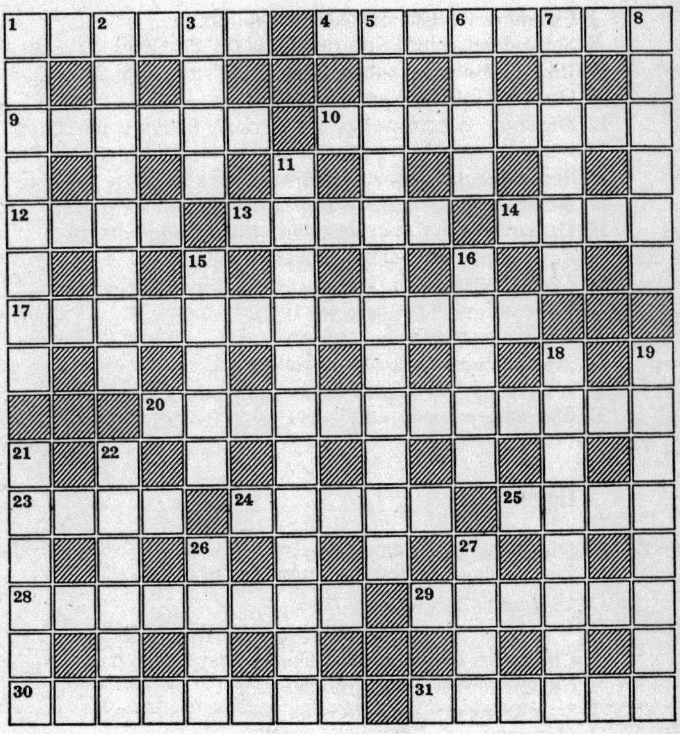

19

Across

1 Preliminary plans for training aviators? (5, 7)
8 Tell-tale renegade in near disorder (7)
9 He can't be aware about Sir Robert's retirement (7)
11 News put out before being cleared (7)
12 Declining to raise a voice about one's family connections (7)
13 Bank robbers usually have them to face (5)
14 Revolting giant who was buried under Mount Etna (9)
16 Formally proposes someone to reform Minnesota (9)
19 A pipe tune held back by the railways (5)
21 Tina with her contrived remedy for stray locks (4-3)
23 Opposed to profit in a way (7)
24 A personal case I open out (7)
25 Stop and go after amber changes (7)
26 A fandango, for instance, numbered among Rome's attractions (7, 5)

Down

1 Fastidious language masters (7)
2 Men who wouldn't think of playing second fiddle? (7)
3 Method of dealing with 24 (9)
4 A hundred requests for bulk containers of wine (5)
5 Changeless ocean flier broaching a brew of ale (7)
6 Completely cleared of the charge? (7)
7 Successful manoeuvre that brought the fellow a first-floor flat? (3-9)
10 A record entry (12)
15 What trawlermen do about a suitable accompaniment for 26 (9)
17 Good vantage-point from which to view the surface of the ocean (7)
18 A girl full of enthusiasm for Chinese dress material (7)
19 André Maurois's prickly English colonel (7)
20 Takes no notice of redeveloped regions (7)
22 He's one in island races with you and me (5)

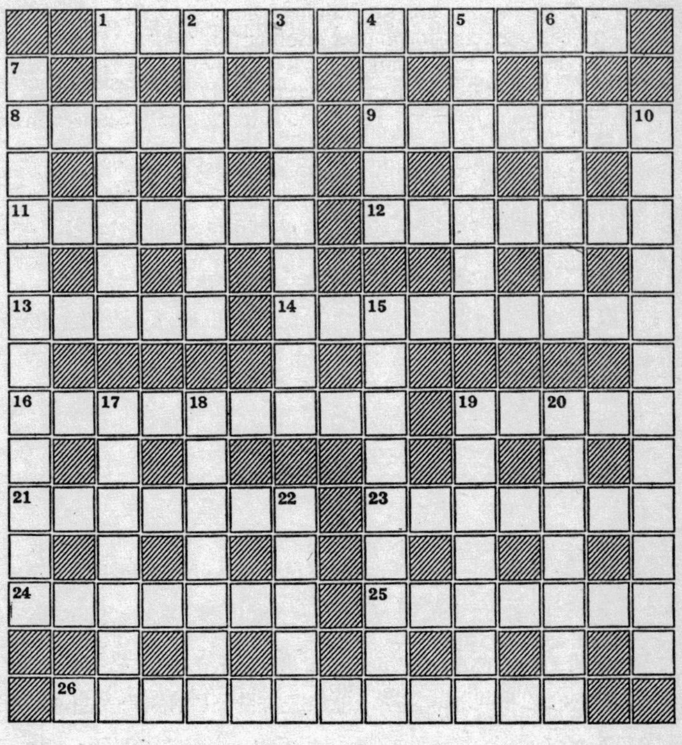

20

Across

1 A drink before the dance. What a thumping idea! (5-4)
9 Threaten chaps with one (6)
10 Proficient employees make a bridge contract easier to get (4, 5)
11 A fellow is a good-looking man (6)
12 Their enthusiasm could possibly shock people (4-5)
13 What a youngster gets into as a result of wild capers (6)
17 Parliamentary do? (3)
19 First offer satisfactory rest is what the courteous host should do (3, 3, 4-5)
20 One who may vote on a current measure (3)
21 Degrees needful if one is to get the right angle on things (6)
25 Following one or two notes, reality is misrepresented in it (5, 4)
26 Gilded bronze (6)
27 They tease a young lady about the boss (9)
28 Sightseer permit provides a loophole (6)
29 In twisting streets they draw attention (9)

Down

2 More suggested what ever fewer think of as politically attainable (6)
3 Select military units not normally scared (6)
4 One might have a crack at it in South America (6)
5 Sewing-bag for a gallant? (6, 9)
6 He begs to repair before admitting personal inability to do so (9)
7 It measures falls by inches (4-5)
8 County redistributed these as retirement cover (3-6)
14 Left a group of players done in (9)
15 Halving it will result in a half or a whole half too (3, 6)
16 This month, above all, the editor is put in his place (9)
17 Ottoman character central to sagas (3)
18 Highest of the first 16 letters (3)
22 Kindergarten revolutionary holds fifty per cent of the recipe (6)
23 Union advice to workers wanting a smoke? (6)

24 The sick and healthy hardly suit (3, 3)

21

Across

1 Kind and impressive letters (4)
3 Motto for the past 1900 odd years (5)
6 Back favourites for pace (4)
11 Old kind of bridge where lots are put up (7)
12 Drawback of T. Carter (7)
13 Air trip cancelled, with any number taken in, for it was only imagination (6, 2, 5)
16 Timber door we'd constructed (7)
17 For example, turning in early as tired men would (7)
18 It may be piled before an entrance (7)
21 A moral danger in anyone's life – a major disaster in mine (7)
23 Get up regulation for committee control, and . . . (8, 5)
26 . . . stick out for the proposal (7)
27 Bring life to a somewhat disturbed inmate (7)
28 Scoundrel more likely to turn over old leaves than new ones (4)
29 Current sources of local Communist activity? (5)
30 Wood on the South Coast (4)

Down

1 Part up, but beware of it (4)
2 About 50 chosen to be preserved (7)
4 Not indeed indicated (7)
5 The highest achievement of mammalian evolution? (7)
7 Army doctors taken in by a sailor – for a ride? (4-3)
8 Devout and sober prime minister (4)
9 One in the forward line holding authority is, of course, an officer (4-9)
10 It makes for ease of cutting in fields and woods (8, 5)
14 A follower takes a journey by horse, accompanied by the groom (5)
15 An acacia tree is everything I own (5)
19 Prospect requiring no insight? (7)
20 A pointed reminder of Scottish Nationalism? (7)
21 Tobacco which puts an end to the swine (7)
22 It is mean to declare how old one is (7)

21

24 Fight which is probably rigged (4)
25 It may be on the menu if the meal is over a pound (4)

22

Across

1 Manet composition about an inspiring female pastime (9)
9 The Arab terrain that makes me turn cross? (7)
10 Any itch will cause her discomposure (7)
11 Some gunner very likely to weaken (7)
12 Courtly splendour put before a grim French courtesan (9)
14 Fresh courage we get when rate is revised (downwards?) (3, 5)
15 Empty vegetables for convivial occasions (6)
17 A spotted deer-stalker? (7)
20 Adventurous old Portuguese king taken in by a group of intriguers (6)
23 Put on too much weight (8)
25 Burning passion (9)
26 Advice on clues treated anagrammatically (7)
27 St Simeon, among others, put it in fashion (7)
28 Perhaps a cabin required for nautical manoeuvres (3-4)
29 Sporting chance of a bite in the Remove at Greyfriars (3-6)

Down

2 Rural dancing centre (7)
3 Determined to attack (3, 4)
4 Sea-food served after the entrée? (4, 4)
5 Net return on a Yorkshire river holding (6)
6 Hiawatha's favourite pub in Maine, complete with sunk fence (9)
7 Considerable distance to drive along? (7)
8 Harassed nurse left with a sense of grievance (9)
13 Not prepared to act? (7)
15 At a loss to explain how publishers' remainders may be disposed of (5, 4)
16 Technically speaking, it means filling a vacancy (9)
18 Puzzling problem I sort out in a cricket club (8)
19 From which one might get late bus – to Lisbon, perhaps? (7)
21 Letters meant to be read with feeling (7)
22 He flies a sextet over a craggy hill (7)
24 Self-possession of the doctor after a ragged cut-off (6)

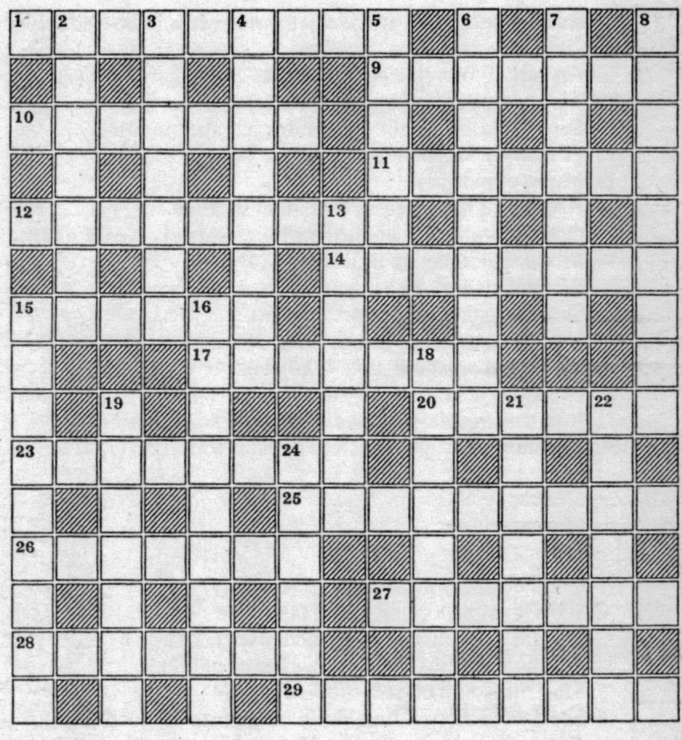

23

Across

1 As an assistant his prime asset would seem to be dexterity (5-4, 3)
8 An early Florentine poet, noted as moderately slow (7)
9 Third estate of communal lands (7)
12 Second-class in drink, but entirely competent (4)
13 Be healthy for suit (5)
14 Music of mirth (4)
17 Redesign a life-saver for Communists all at sea? (7)
18 One from which to judge the whole, formerly plentiful (7)
19 Moral doubt having little weight (7)
22 Where kids may be leathered in North Africa! (7)
24 She's a small type, but precious (4)
25 Coarse material the skilful driver should steer clear of (5)
26 He's the chap about after 12's drink (4)
29 P.S. Ethel changed her name (7)
31 Run true in a devious way to provide nourishment (7)
32 Levelling the social structure by later education (7, 5)

Down

1 Questioned cryptically, and screened (7)
2 Scots go as a working group (4)
3 The amended rate at a specified place (7)
4 Attribute responsibility to a writer of old (7)
5 Mud turned up on soft rubbish heap (4)
6 She devotes herself unselfishly in order to do good (3)
7 Admiralty reticence is an additional force to be reckoned with (5, 7)
10 Otherwise cut down low deck (5)
11 The Ancient Mariner's shipmates? They're key men afloat (8, 4)
15 Was an additional bit of writing having plenty of sting (5)
16 Henry means to worry (5)
20 Again public transport provides pictorial clue (5)
21 Listener afterwards made of clay (7)
22 Stone worker in charge of secret implications (7)
23 Flags and blushes perhaps (7)
27 Eager for an Irish dirge (4)

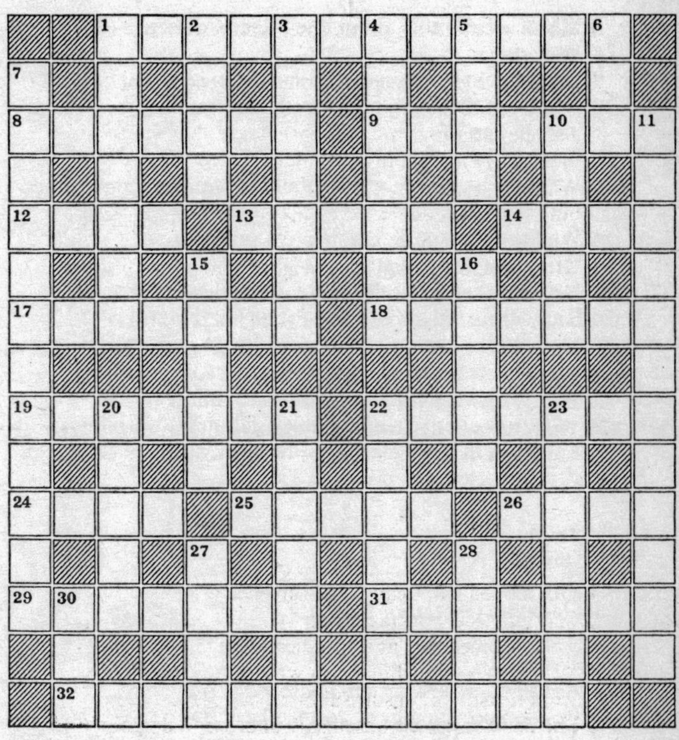

28 Part of a reasonably superficial space (4)
30 The French oriental sheltered side (3)

24

Across

5 Makes a brief note about one's floor supporters (6)
8 Holy orders (5, 3)
9 Caesar went from success to success once he got over it (7)
10 A girl of Marxist sympathies infiltrating the Football Association (5)
11 Extremely flat part of Scotland (9)
13 What the housewife's task should be with the rooms turned out? (8)
14 Wolfish flower spike coming to a point (6)
17 Drink just one round (3)
19 He attends at Cambridge, but doesn't study there (3)
20 Sadly disturbed about end of June hold-ups (6)
23 Members of a select group, possibly (8)
26 All that's required to make cement into concrete (9)
28 West Africa's greatest long-distance runner (5)
29 It flies low after retrospective legislation (7)
30 Engineers in main plans for French city (8)
31 A wild horse rescued by breeches-buoy? (6)

Down

1 Shows no respect for food! (6)
2 An apt voice for the hero in opera who was a wise old Trojan (7)
3 As weird as the Martian landscape? (9)
4 Position occupied by a crowned head (6)
5 A creature that chatters till brought in with perky self-satisfaction? (8)
6 Bad king who was bound to make penal revolutions (5)
7 Fairly large number of handouts (8)
12 Hundred gunners turning round a bend (3)
15 Hills and mountains far from the coast? (2-7)
16 Unmanly drinking habits! (3-5)
18 What the Welsh choir sang as King George put into Hove (3, 5)
21 Wild-cat exploit (3)
22 They can't be 23, poor chaps! (7)
24 The full extent of the rise (6)

24

25 Hazard of crowded city life for which bridge-builders must make allowance (6)

27 The first Norman duke adds nothing to the official record (5)

25

Across

1 Nuclear phenomenon to link with sappers' actual fighting (5, 8)
10 One in a USSR organisation . . . (7)
11 . . . otherwise a Red Com (7)
12 First person mad about a girl (4)
13 Gamble with little between the odds (5)
14 Handy punch maker (4)
17 I 'ad node trouble. Obviously! (7)
18 Strange terrain for a teacher (7)
19 Becomes hard to be ill and go to sea (3, 4)
22 Picture hung as the result of fabricated evidence? (5-2)
24 Time for our pronouncement (4)
25 Thirty-one days on the road apparently (5)
26 Predisposition to be crooked (4)
29 27 not disconcerted in court? (2, 5)
30 Where one goes to train for a position in life (7)
31 A coded paragraph which features in escapist literature? (6, 7)

Down

2 Ill-disposed small house just a step over the fence (7)
3 Talking of bridge, I do not pass in the same place (4)
4 Girl married is taken out again? (7)
5 Old army ensign (7)
6 Egoistic dedication for a book (4)
7 Speech appealing for economy? (7)
8 The education it offers presumably includes language instruction (7, 6)
9 They confer a monopoly on new-type inventions it would seem (7-6)
15 Sex change for Warrant Officer (male)? (5)
16 Commonplace demand of Chicagoans in the 1930s (5)
20 He manages despite corrosion in support of course (7)
21 A tract which ruins all feet (7)
22 Bloomer made by polar explorer with a first-class return (7)
23 The PM, somewhat late, smoothing things out (7)

25

27 That part of familiarity most deserving of contempt (4)
28 Arms deal arrived at by Viking (4)

26

Across

1 Accelerator and choke (8)
5 Health resort anarchist showed mercy? (6)
9 Cooler in a car, and warmer in a house (8)
10 Element of aid represented in past naval spirit (6)
11 Line taken by someone aiming to reduce his circumference about a metre? (8)
12 So lent? Quite otherwise (6)
14 Valentines highly valued by bridge players? (5-5)
18 Skin blemishes are usually all one can see of so-called Negro minstrels (10)
22 Walkers who if (as usual) penniless would find public transport (6)
23 Insignificant irritation caused by a small jumper (8)
24 The ambition of a newly emergent nation to knock someone off? (6)
25 12 months inclined to be unproductive? (4, 4)
26 I have it! (6)
27 Their business should be blooming (8)

Down

1 Harangue one in business (6)
2 Sort of dream North America's brave (3, 3)
3 Then at place in Kent (6)
4 Inspected from the bridge? (6, 4)
6 Price includes bill passed for normal procedure (8)
7 Ridicule a variety of rare lily (8)
8 About Monday God-worship becomes devil-worship (8)
13 It conceals features of matrimonial expectancy (6, 4)
15 True bass arrangement is very deep (8)
16 Somehow amass car oil (8)
17 To omit mention of the giant-killer may amuse the children (8)
19 Way in which a queen of England supported a Frenchman (6)
20 Several who take the plunge (6)
21 Suit beaters (6)

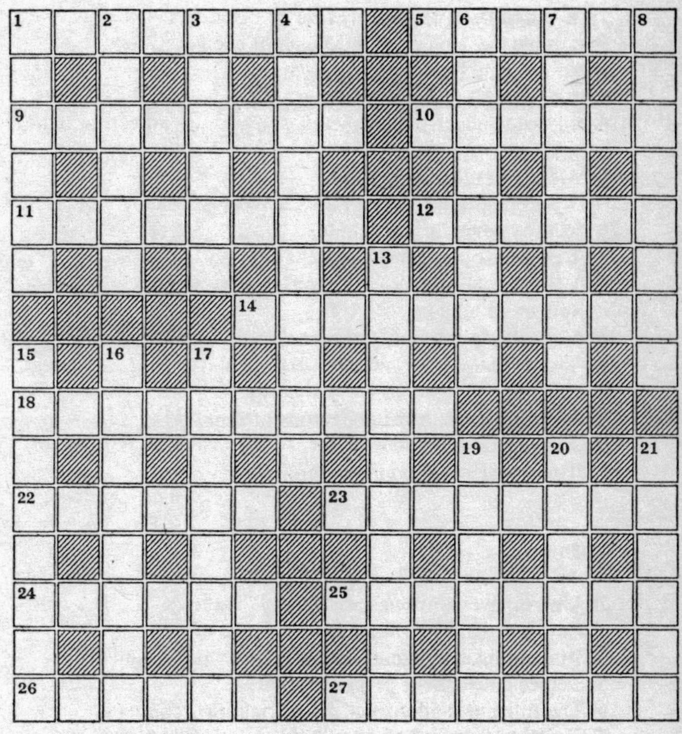

Across

1 Investigator in the family line of business (11)
9 A game old king coming to naught eventually (4)
10 Newly sealed processed cheese (11)
11 In both isn't it one alternative? (4)
14 He needs silver-plated metal, something to keep out the cold (7)
16 Swept by? (7)
17 Unsuccessful day's hunt back in West Africa (5)
18 Secured parity in the field (4)
19 A cliff left by accident, perhaps (4)
20 A ship converted into an Algerian trooper (5)
22 Refuses to take notice? (7)
23 A peculiarly nice and not heartless old fellow (7)
24 A blow that comes suddenly (4)
28 Mark of a completely individual touch (11)
29 Part of Europe now free from restrictions (4)
30 Outrageous treatment of the sacred or not sacred, that is, after disturbance (11)

Down

2 Always revered when pared of colour (4)
3 Permissive midshipman? (4)
4 Sly-looking secessionist leader taking a phone call (7)
5 Deities placed high in the theatre (4)
6 Argentine veils torn over British sailors (7)
7 Sadistic Australian teacher in the outback clearing the way? (4-7)
8 Kindly reset 30 (11)
12 Popular old London mayor striking a blow in new town (11)
13 A prayer placard containing a seabird (11)
15 Short pants? (5)
16 Hot soup swallowed by a graduate who achieved distinction in South Africa (5)
20 Crockery set you don't expect to get at a supermarket (7)
21 It will be for someone else's misfortune that he will hand over protection-money (7)
25 A complaint I'd erased from a guide (4)

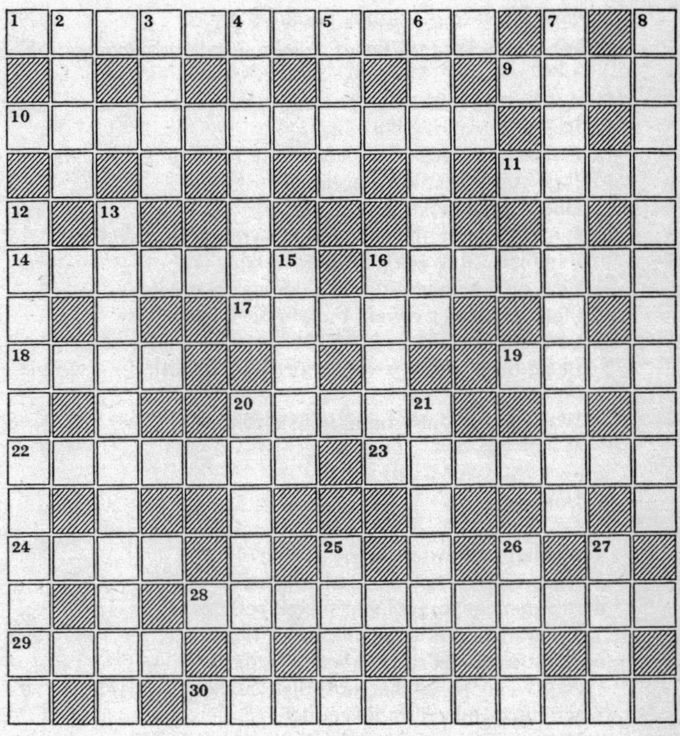

26 Engineers in the Foot may understandably do so! (4)
27 29 ruin (4)

28

Across

1 Those operating it walked to work (9)
8 What an actor may resort to – loose talk or pawning (7-2, 4)
11 Army corps with another back to back (4)
12 Bear a noted loss of means (5)
13 Country to receive first letter from Muhammad Ali (4)
16 It gives me a certain amount (7)
17 One drug to make recompense (7)
18 It oft proclaims the man, Polonius said in *Hamlet* (7)
20 Exploits a little work for the weakling (7)
21 Eggs on a number around Kennington way (4)
22 State Scotland's own in the Middle East (5)
23 Growth of a famous actor (4)
26 Being born with a silver spoon in the mouth, for example (9, 4)
27 Word spread out around in fencing (5-4)

Down

2 Inclination to work in the garden (4)
3 Unspecified article in 23 of course (7)
4 Idly contemplating lunar travel, perhaps (7)
5 Smooth run with a flexible pole (4)
6 Situations one dreams about? (7, 6)
7 Cards run it, bit haphazardly, though there were some serious members on its council! (5, 8)
9 He leads with spirit in a key of two sharps (4-5)
10 R.L.S. told the story, and the youngster dozed off (9)
14 A doubtful sign (5)
15 Bores in the West country (5)
19 Apprentice obviously getting a wage (7)
20 Snare that could give tramp an upset (7)
24 Opinion of half a dozen we look up to (4)
25 One bitter recollection about the essayist (4)

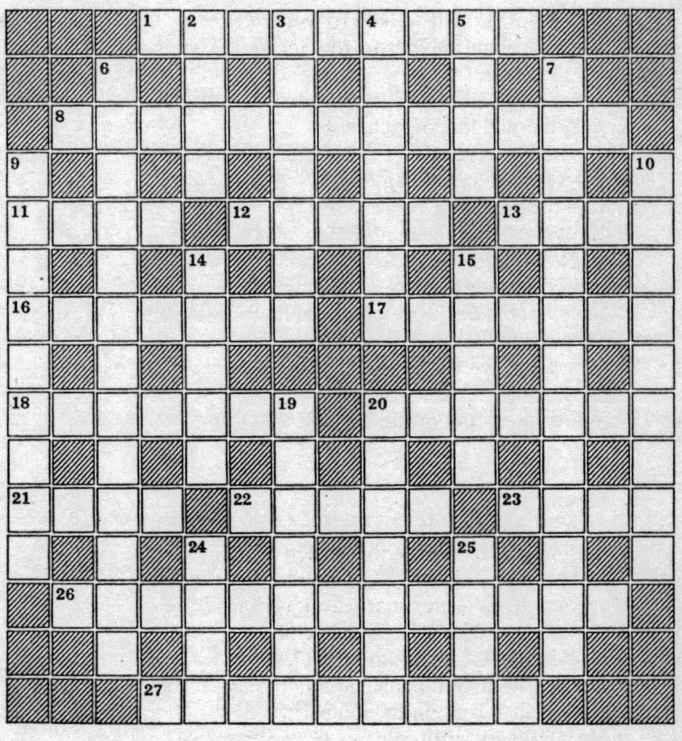

29

Across

8 Quiet Yorkshire stream with no trace of pollution (4)
9 Some food that may be hard to open (3)
10 A badly hurt king whose passing Tennyson lamented (6)
11 Superhuman being who demanded terrible sacrifices of the young (6)
12 In a few written words is French and a hybrid rose (8)
13 One of our earliest poetry books (10, 5)
15 Dickensian Frenchman who had a capital wine business (7)
17 Legal benefit that's cheap at the price! (7)
20 Found guilty of employing Communist labour? (6, 3-6)
23 Madame 15's pointedly revolutionary activity (8)
25 Used language that was abusive, though guarded (6)
26 Great Dane who got wet feet (6)
27 The boy Rex takes on (3)
28 Sin that may give one a shock in retrospect (4)

Down

1 Domed structure put up when coal gets sorted out (6)
2 Hot drink with a fruity flavour (5, 3)
3 How the trains must be run if the railways are to survive! (2, 3, 5, 5)
4 Rise, and in places rising (5, 2)
5 A meeting that should be relatively congenial (6, 9)
6 Arrangement of asters on Lake Maggiore (6)
7 Bet it's a slow-moving boat with square ends! (4)
14 The mentor from whom the infant Samuel imbibed wisdom (3)
16 A time series (3)
18 Not the Jews who give us the low-down on roof coverings (8)
19 Poor reason for inability to purchase a new grey bag (7)
21 Produce sharp words of dismissal (3, 3)
22 The pupil's batting cover? (6)
24 From anyone a tidy verdict (4)

29

30

Across

8 Chant not off key . . . (6)
9 . . . song by drunk – well corked? (8)
10 Salt backward brothers take into the system (6)
11 Demanding task for a debt collector (8)
12 The age of one (3)
13 He does not call, but has a restless night (6)
14 Ideas he introduced among Conservatives, but . . . (8)
16 . . . practical attitude is needed within the sphere of government (7)
18 Lots of games associated with pencils and paper (7)
23 Order into bed in an edgy condition? (8)
27 Oriental setting in which father houses a god (6)
28 Acre minus 100 square metres (3)
29 A metal or I'm much confused (8)
30 Wake up to the sound of thunder (6)
31 German prince confronting his traditional enemy (8)
32 Not celebrated like low mass (6)

Down

1 Singularly uncommon example of multiplication (3, 2, 3)
2 Big deficit in nationalised industry and . . . (8)
3 . . . hell-hound upsetting another such industry in chaotic rescue (8)
4 Abilities portrayed by stories about the Northern Territory (7)
5 Suave in a turban, eh? (6)
6 Giggle coming from sober man in a row (6)
7 Coins proverbially as good as the rest (6)
15 Alternative to a symbol of majesty (3)
17 Anger one army corps (3)
19 Topside? That is what a feller may deliver by hand (5-3)
20 A matrimonial two-timer (8)
21 Reminiscent of accommodation charge swallowing unemployment benefit (8)
22 Very hard worker supporting a mother (7)
24 Not the same backing to the woman's (6)
25 Tired Yeomanry initially confronted by a raised sword (6)

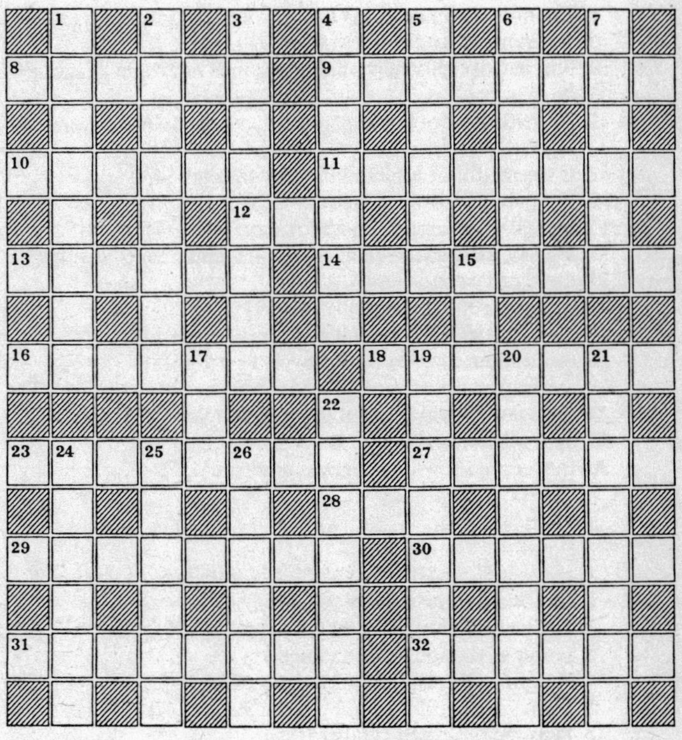

26 Dried fruit is to be found in the rain (6)

31

Across

1 The military engineering profession's call for repeal (10)
6 A very peculiar bloomer (4)
10 Where workers strike while the iron is hot to make money (5)
11 Old food-vendor has apparently swallowed a handy warmer (6-3)
12 It presses for accommodation by the club (4-4)
13 He gives a fellow an alternative (5)
15 Inexplicable false claim about short silver (7)
17 It's lace manufactured for use in undergarments mostly (7)
19 Landlord's characters (7)
21 Moral for the laic organisation (7)
22 Poet who makes a big hit in American sport (5)
24 He is about fifty, in the attic, yet vigorous (8)
27 Rumoured description of what happened on 24/10/45 (9)
28 Rule that would be alien to the F.O. (5)
29 Spare field marshal (4)
30 Innocence shown by spotless workers (5, 5)

Down

1 Craft with prow missing (4)
2 Featherweight fighters may be lit up by it (4, 5)
3 Coffer as the source of a cough (5)
4 Cart from which a tumbler tumbled (7)
5 Aggressive action taken by those insulted (7)
7 Type seen in central Italy (5)
8 Is it unsuitable for compositions of major importance? (5, 5)
9 Common girl goes to city where flappers take the plunge (4-4)
14 Nonetheless revellers may have great times during them (5, 5)
16 Spring-clean – also do a bunk (5, 3)
18 'I can't act, I order action!' (9)
20 It can break rising young men (7)
21 Animal not normally chained (7)
23 Non-uniform exponent of Koranic law (5)

31

25 Heart-broken world (5)
26 Responsibility is apparently ours (4)

32

Across

5 Girl's name for an elastic-sided boot (6)
8 Withdrawal of rural services may compel him to get car put into shape (8)
9 Pretending to interpret is definitely her scene (7)
10 Overdeveloped southern ranges (5)
11 An Asiatic comb Diana treated roughly (9)
13 A simple brew . . . (4-4)
14 . . . on which cider manufacturers base their products (6)
17 Roman rule (3)
19 Two articles suitable for inclusion in literary gossip column (3)
20 Mysterious man who leads a religious sect? (6)
23 What's dad's game? That's what they'll want to see when he goes abroad (8)
26 Sheds not fit for living in? (9)
28 A course in astronomy (5)
29 Expert bricklayer who fought for Scotland's freedom (7)
30 Place in which mirages are seen (5, 3)
31 I break in the front line all for nothing (2, 4)

Down

1 Burn up the miles on the highway (6)
2 Foreign currency that won't buy much in a Cornish resort, right? (7)
3 Victorian maid lovingly invited to go cycling (5, 4)
4 The threat of corporal punishment brought up in the Middle East (6)
5 Early 17th century girl holding a sturdy horse (8)
6 Men of intelligence embarrassed and defiled (5)
7 Errors I bet thousands embrace! (8)
12 Supply weapons to a branch of the fighting services (3)
15 Previously agreed terms of admission (9)
16 German music-master who sounds like a 22 (8)
18 Bewildered centaurs of pre-Roman origin (8)
21 A pie I omitted to copy (3)
22 Snob served with ice and lemon at a wine-party? (7)
24 A vessel with fuel to discharge (6)

32

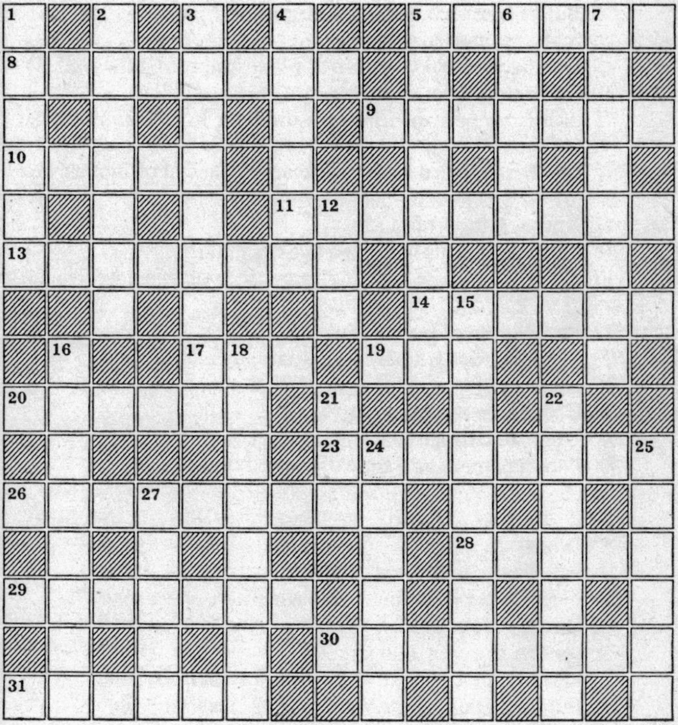

25 Rock adder? (6)
27 Some lethal matter or innocent diversion on board (5)

33

Across

1 But he doesn't win the girl, despite his title (4, 3)
5 Stop the chorus! (7)
9 One doesn't make a summer plant seed round the wall (7)
10 Come out, Oriental fellow, tea's mashed! (7)
11 A former railway company dwelling in charitable home (4-5)
12 Smith is returned to the commanding height of Biblical law (5)
13 Kansas City artifice (5)
15 Lacking 25 cents suggests a fight to a finish (2, 7)
17 and 19 Otherwise as daft as a goose is sufficient equivalent (2, 4, 2, 1, 5)
22 Perfect type of tradesman's slogan? (5)
23 Ingredient for Chinese soup that may include eggs (5-4)
25 Hazards of course – but do they commonly run away? (7)
26 Chaps turn it on to refer to (7)
27 Unreliable Eric is about to desert (7)
28 Ivan ran amok in a state of blessed oblivion (7)

Down

1 Fleet-footed flyer commonly wrecked a short road (7)
2 Having weapons with points on, moved together like bees (7)
3 Left in much protective mixture for roots (5)
4 But it's old money here in the S.W. Pacific (3, 6)
5 About the first woman magistrate long ago (5)
6 Make a signal to personnel to uphold the standard (9)
7 Opposed to a profit, good man! (7)
8 To want that is right, though comparatively broke? (7)
14 Let oil men combine in a softening product (9)
16 Hunter after his prey cuts slate or stone (9)
17 Can I provide a friendly solution? (7)
18 He didn't say 'Lend me your ears'; he gathered them (7)
20 Air came deviously to the continent (7)
21 Ain't it a mix-up for a dreamy queen? (7)
23 Graduate so essential (5)
24 Norse alternative for Spanish title (5)

33

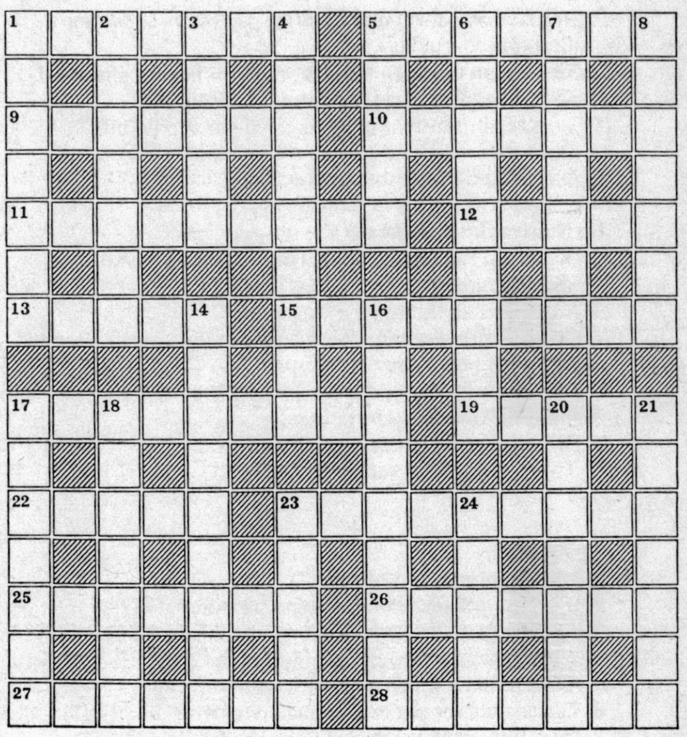

34

Across

1 He may not feel so great when the psychiatrist has done with him! (12)
8 Frenchman who painted a brook breaking out afresh (7)
9 The name misapplied for a hazard of mine (7)
11 Type of aircraft that requires three pick-up points (7)
12 The outside of a fruit pie served incorrectly with fish (7)
13 A vegetable I follow on and on (5)
14 Person who thrives on butchery (4-5)
16 Clearly not the sphere of the imagination (4, 5)
19 Organised tour round small river city in Cornwall (5)
21 The flags that have the unions cornered? (7)
23 A mongrel apparently lacking poise (7)
24 Comparatively obscure round-the-world traveller I pursue with little hesitation (7)
25 Highland war-cries heard at intervals on the commercial channel (7)
26 Happy to arrange the right deal (5-7)

Down

1 Market in one kind of rifle (7)
2 Bygone craft everyone has gone crazy about (7)
3 A wild-cat strike could do him serious harm (4-5)
4 What Mary may be called in Maryland? (5)
5 A salt container taken up with ceremony (7)
6 Tireless worker under a barrage not giving an inch (7)
7 Do what you like, you can, if you're a tailor! (4, 8)
10 Imported cordage material reclassified as sports gear (7, 5)
15 Part of Spain and the country that has bases there inter alia (9)
17 One of the points of Zulu militarism (7)
18 Droll shaking movement followed by a frenzied sigh (7)
19 Happen to play for a team, maybe (4, 3)
20 Such melodies, according to Keats, are sweeter (7)
22 A rash sort of girl (5)

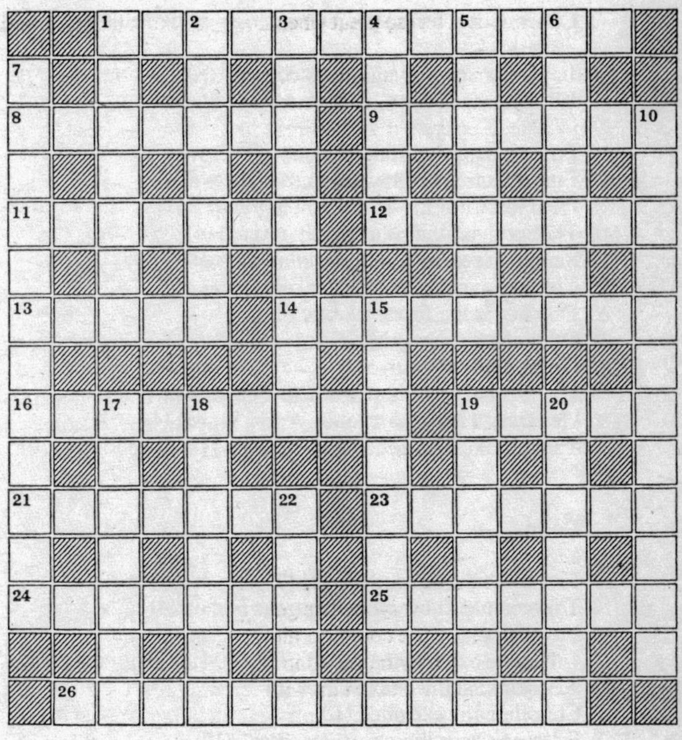

35

Across

1 Court action brought only to satisfy pride helps the lady make up (6-4)
6 In current form is sure to make record (4)
9 Hard hit by rackets, it does not always finish up in court (6-4)
10 Pure constitution for a country (4)
13 Fine direction to one making advances (7)
15 Coin tossed to me would add to mine! (6)
16 The survivor who is endlessly revered (6)
17 Simply die to vote with the winning side (4, 3, 8)
18 The assets in which they deal are frozen (6)
20 Don't pass the French fabric (6)
21 Of name AL, not AML (7)
22 Better office of course (4)
25 The captain and his vessel held by a teacher (10)
26 Herb was a field marshal in World War II (4)
27 The mistake is in sober men becoming panic-mongers (10)

Down

1 Five one-time Army girls holding lots of liquor (4)
2 They should know whose son was Joshua (4)
3 Toy dish (6)
4 Otherwise can't be in time, sir, for a PM appointment (7, 8)
5 Article replacing one in silver (6)
7 Conditionally excluded (10)
8 Fellow citizens in non-urban areas? (10)
11 Incoherent, like one whose leg has been pulled too hard (10)
12 Chance of a flat which doesn't go with the key? (10)
13 Struck south with winter protection on hand (7)
14 Taking away, though half remain on the cricket ground (7)
19 Childhood start of every nonagenarian (6)
20 More ostensibly just a shade lighter (6)
23 So clumsily shut (4)
24 Preparation of soup means work (4)

Across

1 Casual role served by prisoners (4-4)
5 Thrashed for being stuck up? (6)
9 Parasitic example of the devoted listener to recordings? (8)
10 Slow movement (6)
11 He travels overseas to get home (8)
13 Charge put back for the rest? (4, 2)
14 Sound organ (3)
16 Admission made by a hundred in cases reviewed (6)
19 Complaint from which to die swallowing vast quantities of water (7)
20 Its ends, though poles apart, are equally attractive (6)
21 But upset it still holds water (3)
26 His alternatives were to escape Bumble or live in (6)
27 Renegade advice to one who can't afford new apparel (8)
28 The result of adding ten to the score (6)
29 Most impressive type of industrial action (8)
30 Rulers all at sea? (6)
31 Does it imply no shipping charges for property? (8)

Down

1 One who encourages glib talk? (6)
2 Fix up a couple of engineers maybe (6)
3 Tractors built with a view to the landscape? (6)
4 Serviceman right in an American State (6)
6 The house in which royalty receive visitors (8)
7 Not apart from the aim of rival suitors (8)
8 Commissionaire's job perhaps, on which something hinges (8)
12 Maybe call for a partner or overcall a partner (4, 3)
15 Ailment that doesn't appear to affect health (3)
16 A provider of transport on sea and land (3)
17 One who has no end of a living (8)
18 In this day and age, it's something to be switched on, for a start (8)
19 Legionnaire who leaves the Sahara with hesitation? (8)
22 Is he always raising objections to fat? (6)
23 Conclusion I've gathered from the vegetable patch (6)

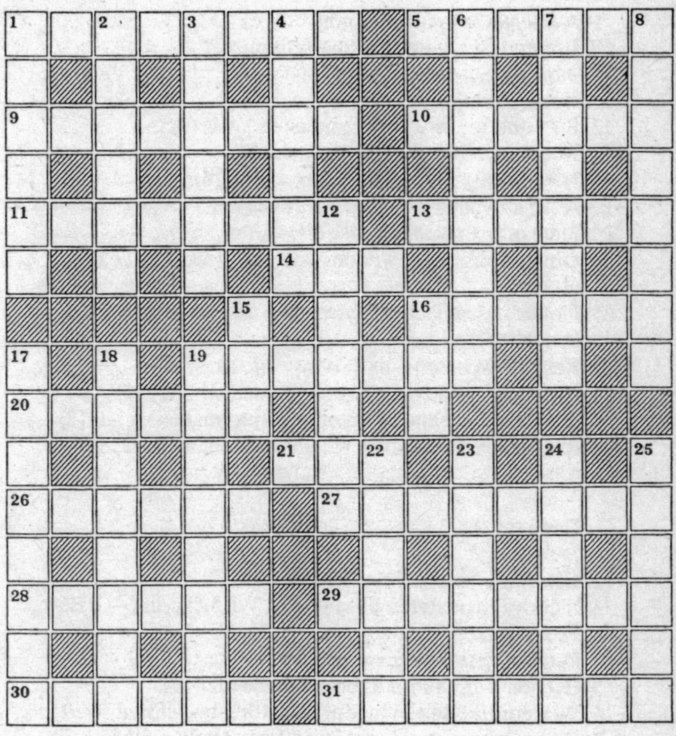

24 Usually it is spotted by numbers at the masked ball (6)
25 Having done some coaching once, put on a play (6)

37

Across

1 A woman who is fairly grey? (3, 6)
9 It reminds fellows to tack on to me (7)
10 Superficially worn down (7)
11 Horace Walpole's down-at-heel castle in Italy (7)
12 Bird duets thrown into confusion? Yes (9)
14 Representative of something else (8)
15 Hibernating snake has shelter within (6)
17 A little bounder that isn't yet one (7)
20 State of my rambling rose (6)
23 Union decision on whether the play deck may be used? (4-4)
25 I offer a serenade, maybe, to a girl employed in a glue factory (9)
26 Relatively patronising (7)
27 An oddly lined worm with a segmented body (7)
28 A solvent civil engineer coming in to make amends (7)
29 Rest assured the waiter will do as I advise! (4, 2, 3)

Down

2 Gives in presents for consideration? (7)
3 'Thou need na start awa sae hasty, Wi' bickering—' (Burns: *To a Mouse*) (7)
4 Past the best time for eating? (8)
5 Get some ideas into a form, maybe (6)
6 Wickedness? I'm in favour of getting by without it (9)
7 How vacuous people act in an East Anglian diocese (7)
8 Progressive automobile show (9)
13 Old retired Jews who shared out their property (7)
15 Huge crushers Canada's crazy on internally (9)
16 Uplift one can find in a housing plan that's . . . (9)
18 . . . the height of distinction? (8)
19 Man gifted with foresight to support the reformation (7)
21 Kind of champagne foolish sappers turn in (7)
22 From across in Italy his noted works became famous (7)
24 Just the thing to secure admittance (6)

37

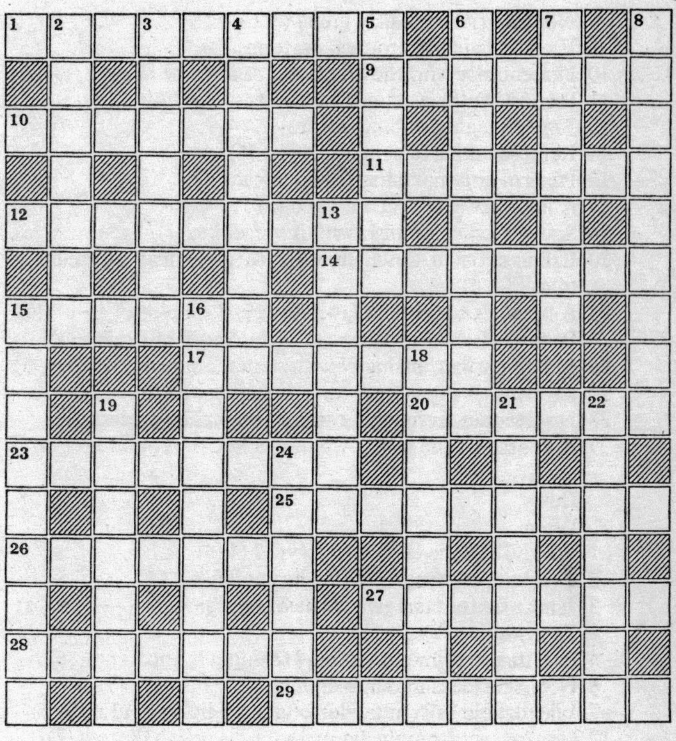

38

Across

6 Good spirit in the play (13)
8 Falstaff's ancient trouble-shooter? (6)
9 Not equipped for the grind of a past Prime Minister facing the gallery (8)
10 Attic salt withal? Not half! (3)
11 Levels at skills seen in retrospect (6)
12 Piece of sirloin competitively priced? (8)
14 Companion also in command (7)
16 Ascetic top columnist, with it in fashion (7)
20 Exhortation to the Chancellor to give local customers a treat? (4, 4)
23 A fistful in anger can play havoc (6)
24 Backward-looking character in the South of France (3)
25 Momentarily train badly with something to slip on (2, 1, 5)
26 Ethereal as Prospero's servant sounds (6)
27 Disease that largely develops in tropical countries (13)

Down

1 Was it the wine talking in Egypt? (4, 4)
2 Resolute law-breaker in the beginning (8)
3 Time's up for changing momentum (7)
4 Really at home with the act (6)
5 Her 10 somehow passes the washing test apparently (6)
6 North American banker martyred for his faith (5, 8)
7 Like the old informer released for a field-day? (3, 3, 2, 5)
12 City excerpt from the lyric (3)
15 Good investment for a pound? (3)
17 Two sailors in charge will be bitter (8)
18 Unhealthy condition I relish, oddly enough, about five (8)
19 Place Salerno in confusion elsewhere (7)
21 Sandwich course, as it were (6)
22 Prophet a high priest has reformed (6)

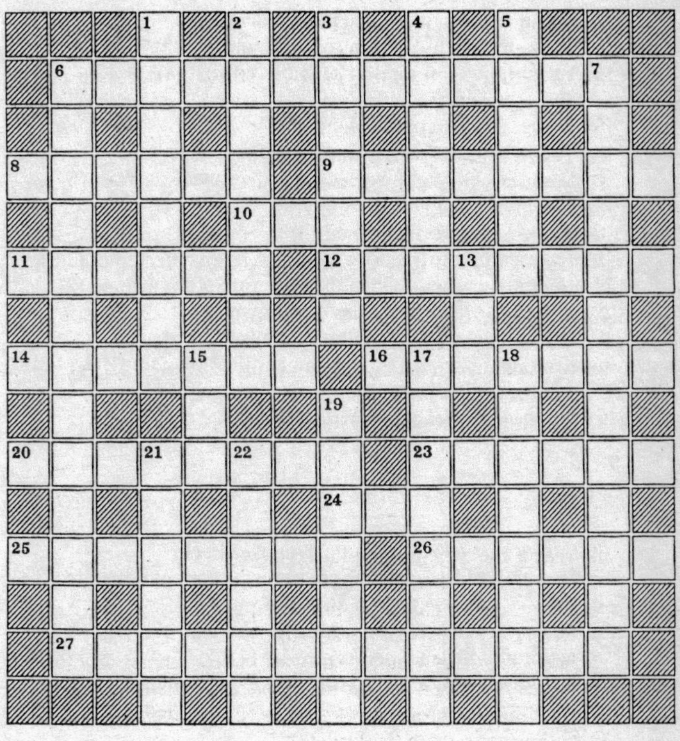

39

Across

1 Stupid fellows that mused on reform (6-5)
8 Examine in detail a plan to use a tunnel? (2, 7, 2)
11 A multiplicity of ducks north of Oxford! (4)
12 Canterbury one, maybe (4)
13 Health check wrongly claimed (7)
15 A fault that makes me tired out in retrospect (7)
16 Answers one might expect from the indecisive poet (5)
17 Some return of gin (4)
18 Hook-worm, for instance? (4)
19 Enjoy complete freedom of speech as an entertainer (2-3)
21 Picks up new heart when the General Staff is around (7)
22 A paid informer in a class of his own? (7)
23 The burden of love Apollo rejected (4)
26 He is held back by the regional authority (4)
27 A second reason for giving a prison sentence? (5, 2, 4)
28 Innocent ringleaders cryptically defined by 1 (4-7)

Down

2 Empty sort of pun about a preposition (4)
3 Capital goddess breaking number of commandments (7)
4 Time of day when most strikes occur? (4)
5 Their job is to provide power for industry (7)
6 A thing of little value I point out (4)
7 Bird raced by someone else outside my province (3, 2, 6)
8 Wig poor duet but revision shows much better judgement (4, 5-2)
9 Hospitable invitation one couldn't instantly go and accept in days gone by? (5, 6)
10 Dictator of no great importance (5, 6)
14 The place where long-hops may be belted! (5)
15 Record that one is in arrears (5)
19 London club magazine (7)
20 Join the coven, as sirens do (7)
24 The one and only course after soup perhaps (4)
25 Feeling the effects of a beating in tennis or épée practice (4)
26 A border rising, or the Moslem ruler to quell it, possibly (4)

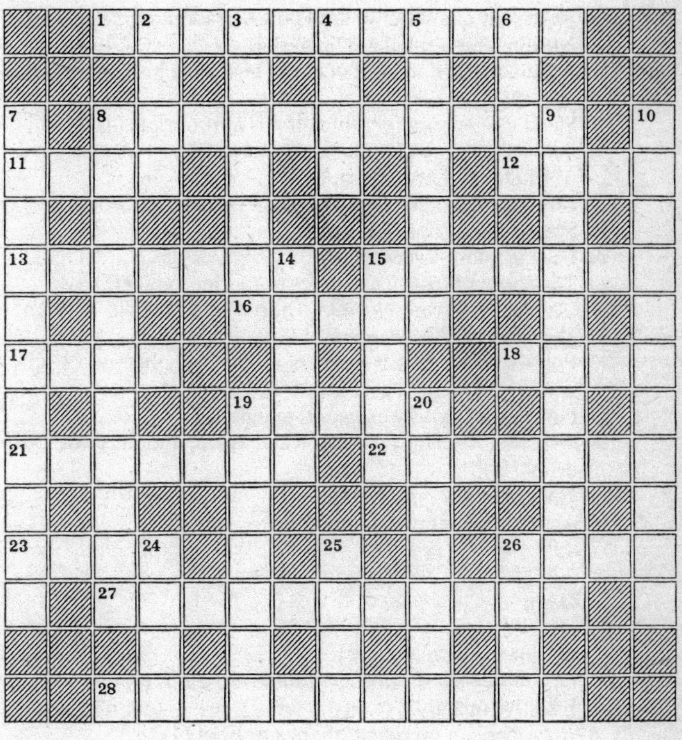

Across

1 Statement of a sober note to police headquarters? (11)
9 Nothing but a Japanese fighter (4)
10 Absolute description of one who has failed his examination (11)
11 Short car journey for which top is appropriate (4)
14 Beloved heroine of a sea rescue story (7)
16 Cardinal Paul holds back (7)
17 Dance which makes a girl from the States go to work (5)
18 Stand against one objection (4)
19 Betting about to cease (4)
20 They are impressive examples of marine agility (5)
22 'And his — were gleaming in purple and gold' (Byron: *Destruction of Sennacherib*) (7)
23 Point to petty officer gunners in the Navy before a Highlander (7)
24 No hit with wife-seekers, seemingly (4)
28 What the Romans built again and again, and once without delay (11)
29 Undiluted bull, maybe! (4)
30 Arrange the score with art (11)

Down

2 A wine guys can hold (4)
3 Ornithological specimens in some museums (4)
4 Effective recital (7)
5 An American president, thanks to Foot (4)
6 Dance which doesn't get anybody very far (7)
7 It goes down with the cold, and up with the 'flu (11)
8 Teller's window providing blanket cover? (11)
12 Progress soundly signified promotion (11)
13 A planner who may get the huff (11)
15 Storms that, headed off, could still be brewing (5)
16 Turns over the lists (5)
20 The part of a car which has not been scratched in a race (7)
21 They are likely to be used with soap cakes (7)
25 The way a psychopath ends (4)
26 Where prisoners begin to wake up? (4)

40

27 Quick way to lose weight (4)

41

Across

1 Sailed without sails from the Middle East instead (7)
5 What the Duke of York's men first had to do come All Fool's Day (5, 2)
9 They literally gave a general help surrounded by charts, though hot-heads (7)
10 Dog cart? (7)
11 Flatten a soccer star? One cannot do more (5, 4)
12 Forming sober habits (5)
13 The wars that could have been nipped in the bud? (5)
15 A tin medal ordered to be plated (9)
17 The top rises stranded seamen can count on (4, 5)
19 A means of current escape which sustains us (5)
22 It will shortly be available from the weavers (5)
23 He imagines he is worth a crown (9)
25 Unfriendly little house with no gate? (7)
26 Where low lags somehow once finished up (7)
27 It is more appreciated in wine than in books (7)
28 A gay bird got up before everyone retired (7)

Down

1 One who has a taste for a bit of embroidery (7)
2 I've cut the top and bottom for the salad (7)
3 Everything I possess has its roots in Australia (5)
4 Died holding a charm, and driven away (9)
5 Strength that lacks decisiveness? (5)
6 Ordering a replant of American flower (3, 6)
7 Henry and I only fish (7)
8 Well read childless person employed (7)
14 Country within the orbit of Russian influence? (9)
16 His job is to take note (9)
17 The hold is covered but the chickens are out! (7)
18 Dispute wins approval (7)
20 Neat description of a Communist election? (7)
21 Prophet takes in Navy on the Yorkshire coast (7)
23 The crowd in Fleet Street, for example (5)
24 English essayist from Lisle originally (5)

41

42

Across

1 Woe betide the man he catches stealing a priceless work of art! (9)
8 Picturesque but uncomfortable way to jog along (7, 6)
11 Evade the issue of a field division? (5)
12 Part of a bagpipe that doesn't work (5)
13 Dandy turn still seen on the seat-front in Blackpool (5)
16 Something not often found except in the higher reaches of the atmosphere (6)
17 In a crime-busting organisation and honest, too (6)
18 He makes the Sappers go right back (5)
19 Positionally entitled to be a shot-firer? (6)
20 He cuts a new red stick (6)
21 Sheer robbery, as far as prices are concerned! (5)
24 Untidily amassed? (5)
26 A growing group of sound opposition to robbers (5)
27 Swimming hazard that can give one a big shock (6, 7)
28 The flower to soak when Murphy's out and about (9)

Down

2 Ring me about the training system for this game (5)
3 Transfix the joint made by Wesker (6)
4 Two Poles cutting a tree for a saintly archbishop (6)
5 Ghastly old city breaking cover (5)
6 The excellent chances of success that mountain resorts offer (4, 9)
7 Supplementary fare for the diner? (6, 7)
9 The daily cuppa isn't what she's responsible for, however (9)
10 Having bright little pupils? (5-4)
13 Revolutionary bands expected to do thousands of miles (5)
14 A wild glen where two planes meet (5)
15 What the men going back in 18 do about credit. Not much, that is! (5)
22 He leaves the 14 to get into a state of confusion (6)
23 All that's required to repel one – how horrible! (6)
25 A flower that could well be open before the end of July (5)
26 Four hundred odd Greeks live there (5)

42

43

Across

1 From August 12 to December 10, when complaints may be registered (6, 6,)
9 Once again rent free (7)
10 Hero-worshipper who drowned (7)
11 Nominally vain disposition of 25 (4)
12 Inclines to scenes of contest (5)
13 Stable business (4)
16 Their work may present knotty problems resulting in rags (7)
17 Musical twist for a snake in the grass (7)
18 Complaining about fencing? (7)
21 Run away and sink the ship (7)
23 How to starve expeditiously (4)
24 The monarch in borrowed garments (5)
25 East European bondsman lacking final direction (4)
28 Rare use can be made of such obliteration (7)
29 Brief conical shape (7)
30 'Time, gentlemen, please!' Oh, shut up! (7, 5)

Down

1 A lady's escort must be chivalrous (7)
2 Surrey's ellipsoidal H.Q. (4)
3 A grouping of coin on direction (7)
4 Ceremonial greetings from Salvation Army music-makers (7)
5 A mother for him who never had one (4)
6 The ancient with the scythe in the past (3-4)
7 Regiment of the line, no doubt ready for a brush with the enemy in 1914 (7, 6)
8 Punctual court delivery the customer often looks for in vain (6, 7)
14 Scottish island gunman (5)
15 He was able to watch 50 times better than most (5)
19 Put in place in stable accommodation (7)
20 Fish-pin (7)
21 The superficial justice of Shakespeare (7)
22 Special aptitudes for money once (7)

26 Refuses to recognise reductions (4)
27 Evidence of one of 26 could come from wrecking cars (4)

44

Across

1 One of the few to whom power-sharing is anathema (8)
5 Horses able to pull heavy loads all over the country (6)
9 Damaging impression about an old rebel leader of degenerate character (8)
10 Quickly put what was left in the Post Office (6)
11 They were patient advisers on social welfare (8)
12 Write off about a Christmas publication, maybe (6)
14 The country wedding that made 8 look to Westminster for guidance (3, 2, 5)
18 Climber of a sort in North Devon (10)
22 A girl of fate to achieve parity in sport (6)
23 Lead door ordered in place of gold (2, 6)
24 A reveller wouldn't show his face at such an entertainment (6)
25 One in the church – as a career, presumably (8)
26 Liquor that is diluted and cast out (6)
27 Anguished sea-dog shaken up about Uister (8)

Down

1 An actor who has ranted for years in Lancashire? (6)
2 What I expect from industry once I'm rehabilitated! (6)
3 Burning for a new trend (6)
4 One who undertakes to supply and fix a condenser, possibly (10)
6 Hurried into the foreign seat of government to deliver a vehement address (8)
7 Sinister holy man who claimed to know what was good for the Cesarewitch (8)
8 Part of the UK where there's a call for new government tax to come down! (8)
13 William over-indulging about what he expects to get as the star of the show (3, 7)
15 Shining spectacles of night life in Victorian times? (3-5)
16 Where every man Jack had to go to learn craftsmanship (3, 2, 3)
17 Corpulent guide somehow in need of a rest (8)

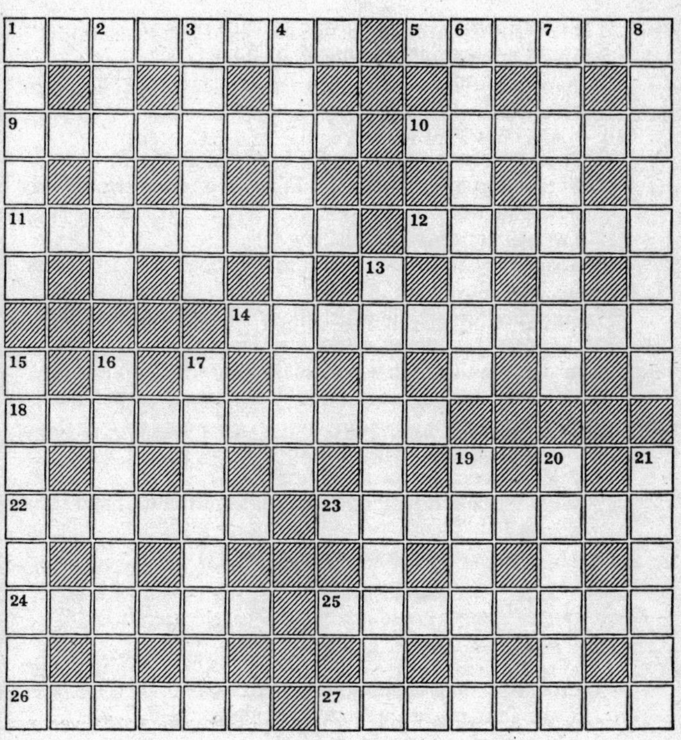

19 Frenchman who won fame by writing on fluid that may heal (6)
20 The insect that makes humanity sit up (6)
21 Quickly achieved the heights without flapping? (6)

45

Across

1 Fewer alternatives for the counterparts of 16 (7)
5 Stuff that floats here and there by noon (7)
9 'Though I am a native here, And — — — —' (*Hamlet*, Act 1) (2, 3, 6, 4,)
10 Right to help an attack (4)
11 Produced, for example, in the Board of Trade (5)
12 Actor suggesting the Pied Piper was only temporarily successful? (4)
15 Two supporters within the law (7)
16 Temporary residents, but hardly enough for a workers' colony (7)
17 Stage performance in which those who co-operate act (7)
19 Choice extract preserved for tea? (4, 3)
21 A German title with which Shakespeare was familiar (4)
22 Short cut to being caught out by the wicket-keeper, maybe (5)
23 One old copper beaten in court (4)
26 Personal bodyguards in service? (7, 8)
27 What the bells do after the best man has put his hand in his pocket? (4, 3)
28 The bishop's position is to supervise (7)

Down

1 Procrastinating suggestion to a tiro on the side (7)
2 Scene-shifters are apparently getting going (7, 2, 6)
3 About to ring a parson up (4)
4 Grand kind of home for a good man at Ely (7)
5 Discover that the visit is abortive? (4, 3)
6 Sound alternatives to sails, perhaps (4)
7 Game men's habits (8-7)
8 What many a gardening chap sure scatters (7)
13 John's up. Maybe he couldn't (5)
14 Hideou- -ose (5)
17 One who applauds a bellringer (7)
18 The line to take to beat the fellow (7)
19 Small Italian wind instrument (7)
20 In fashion it's design that counts with her (7)

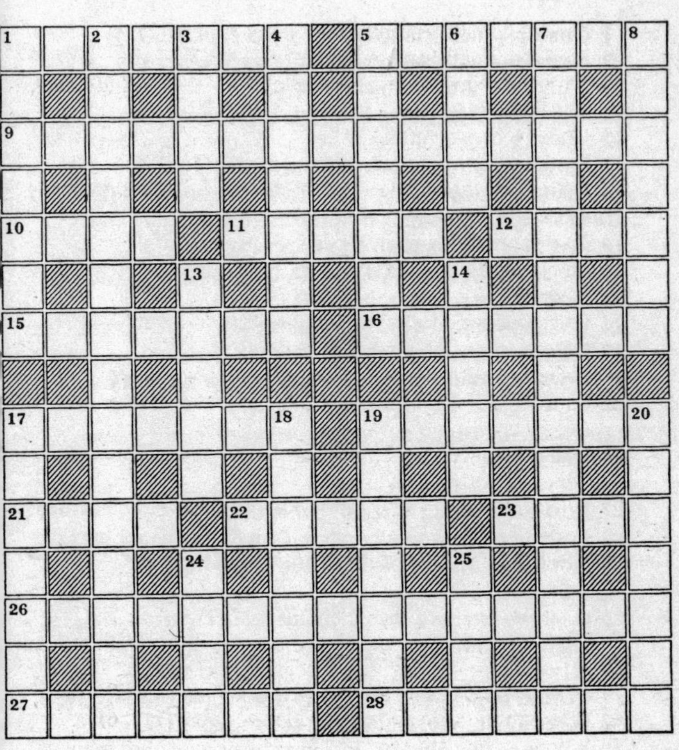

24 It may be cooked by turning up the gas ring (4)
25 Adds pronouncement with cutting potential (4)

Across

1 Guarding successfully against a pickpocket? (7, 5)
8 It moves many to honour a writer before you and me (7)
9 Climbs like American currency (7)
11 Famous actress young Sidney doesn't take off (7)
12 Show contempt of French spies' organisation (7)
13 Mother won round one of her own sex (5)
14 Neat prose translation useful to internationalists (9)
16 Lifelike, and certainly down to earth (9)
19 One who gets his teeth into things (5)
21 Sis isn't to be disturbed, in fact, refuses to budge (7)
23 Drafted like soldiers on parade (5, 2)
24 Refuse to describe the sartorial era (7)
25 Suppose one mine contains silver (7)
26 How a dissolute, inaccurate pace bowler plays? (4, 3, 5)

Down

1 Realm where dog mixes with mink (7)
2 Turning me over to schoolboy Tom to give a tanning (7)
3 Not to be put off, tailed 21 with 10 inside (9)
4 Piano for $1,000 (5)
5 One who blames a metric enthusiast? (7)
6 Send off American servicemen turning up in Connecticut (7)
7 Central heating as a homely first welcome to guests (5-7)
10 Is her job to type, sort out or gather pens? (12)
15 Advice to itinerant dentist feared by private offenders (4-5)
17 A number leaving Australia for another country (7)
18 Time for no delay? (7)
19 In the Costa Brava don't swagger (7)
20 Ten confounded lies capable of being extended (7)
22 Forbidding end (5)

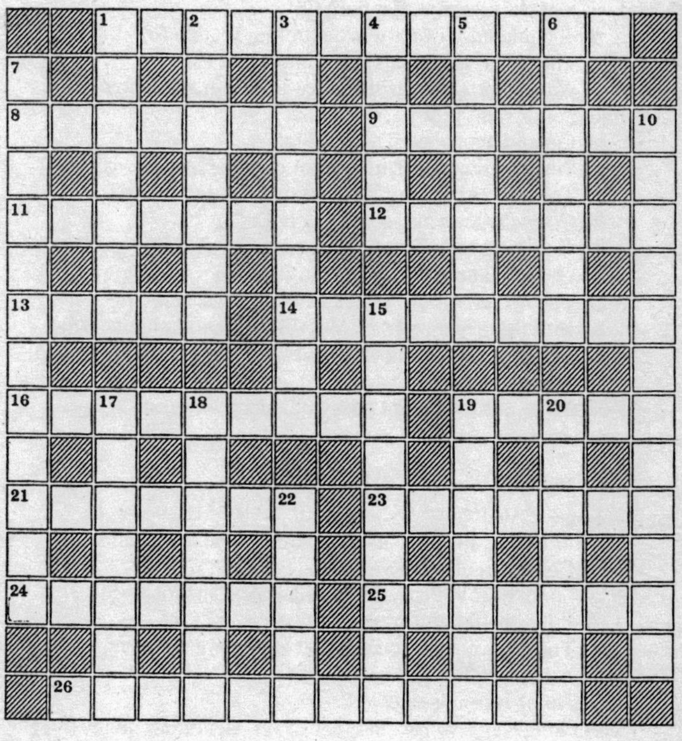

47

Across

1 Get the measure of a bore (9)
9 A conference of natives disrupting Ibadan (6)
10 The urban guerrilla's fighting defence (9)
11 An Asiatic cardinal shrouded in gloom, somehow (6)
12 Sailor saint in waterproof cover (9)
13 Go and get to work again (6)
17 Silver article held in great respect in the Moslem world (3)
19 The Marxist worker representing Ulster? (3, 4)
20 Comic fellow taking nothing back (7)
21 Got one's teeth into some meat every day (3)
23 Out and about under foreign skies (6)
27 The flower a foolish gatecrasher comes back after (9)
28 Bird no longer seen in a Scottish mountain lament (6)
29 Versatile New York team outwardly out of their wits (4-5)
30 Money obtained by letter (6)
31 Mentions a different part of the Middle West (9)

Down

2 Not good in singular articles, but oil is its product (6)
3 Force an entry? (6)
4 Small firm in Peru out to make good the losses (6)
5 Putting straight upset dignity (7)
6 The share of the proceeds that goes to the Government (6, 3)
7 A huge ball in ridiculous shape (9)
8 Habit-forming activity (9)
14 Mendicant winger that thrives on Australian honey (5-4)
15 It embellishes a point about Royal Navy men (9)
16 Craft that relies for its effectiveness on fundamental duplicity (9)
17 The girl out of 2 (3)
18 One service there's no chance of getting back (3)
22 I'm surrounded by battered paint drums (7)
24 Pencil study penetrated by a gleam of light (6)
25 Not the hills one has designs about (6)
26 A code of laws to assimilate (6)

47

48

Across

7 Even so, someone must pull its trigger (9)
8 Cereal disease has the work unit turning to (5)
10 One of the big cats at Oxford, it sounds (5, 3)
11 Decoration a king has on in fairy-land (6)
12 Head cook's delicacy (4)
13 Description of the lesser evil? (3, 2, 3)
15 and 17 Being in contention great shouting can make all but the final point (7, 3, 4)
20 Only one sock? (4-4)
22 Is it a dagger one sees before you, Mr Bogarde? (4)
25 He plays a bit so nothing's complicated (6)
26 Two fish hold the key to a dilettantish practice (8)
27 Meeting a friend by the river (5)
28 As famous last words are recorded, incidentally? (2, 7)

Down

1 Give the horse a tidy hot meal (5)
2 Thus a colour recalled a musical composition (6)
3 Temple of the Greek god switched on (8)
4 and 19 It should be a brilliant celebration (7, 7)
5 After-dinner treat for imbibers in Illinois (8)
6 O, such a lot is ruined by it! (9)
9 Left half of 5 (4)
14 Norfolk vegetable? (5-4)
16 Do brunettes so react without reason? (8)
18 Butler hero with whom I'd a brush possibly (8)
19 See 4
21 Fragments of a different sort (4)
23 Get pleasure from a condiment (6)
24 Unknown to a girl (5)

48

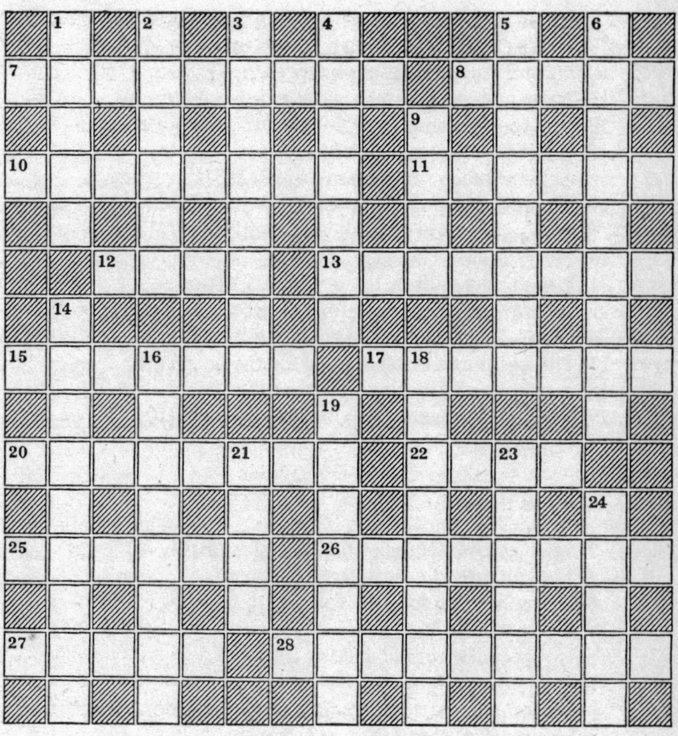

49

Across

1 Harsh corollary for a dare-devil who is taken aback? (5-5)
9 Untrustworthy person who turns to abuse (4)
10 A solid lens made everywhere (2, 3, 5)
11 To a small mountain it is but a tiny creature (6)
12 One way of drinking a North European gin cocktail (7)
15 Broken lyre set in a nutshell (7)
16 Achieve success in the long run? (2, 3)
17, 18 and 7 down The nursery rhyme girl who didn't fancy tucking into beef or pork, apparently (4, 3, 1, 6, 4)
19 The criminal is sore (5)
21 Place to get fruit or tea by the way (7)
22 Where the price is paid for going on a ring-road? (4-3)
24 Leggy youngsters left in rocky hollows (6)
27 The midshipman who called for the hunt? (10)
28 A backward French wall flower (4)
29 An undergarment tried out and ridiculed (10)

Down

2 Satisfies nine-tenths of the law, presumably (4)
3 The top rate of course for a 1 across? (6)
4 Doing nothing to cause further irritation? (7)
5 Frivolous act for a queen who came to a tragic end (4)
6 He specialises in illicit stock transfers (7)
7 See 17 across
8 Tolerably good verdict about a nice-looking conifer? (6, 4)
12 Unshapely piece of fashionable material (4, 2, 4)
13 Package split by a South American alchemist who provoked great hostility (10)
14 The sand around him may, if the matador is (5)
15 Picture card from the sailor to return (5)
19 She has to worry about a flood of water (7)
20 Eminent lord swallowing vulgar gratitude (7)
23 Free to re-do some seamy work? (3, 3)
25 Atmosphere broken with a song (4)
26 One may cross it in a steamer easily (4)

49

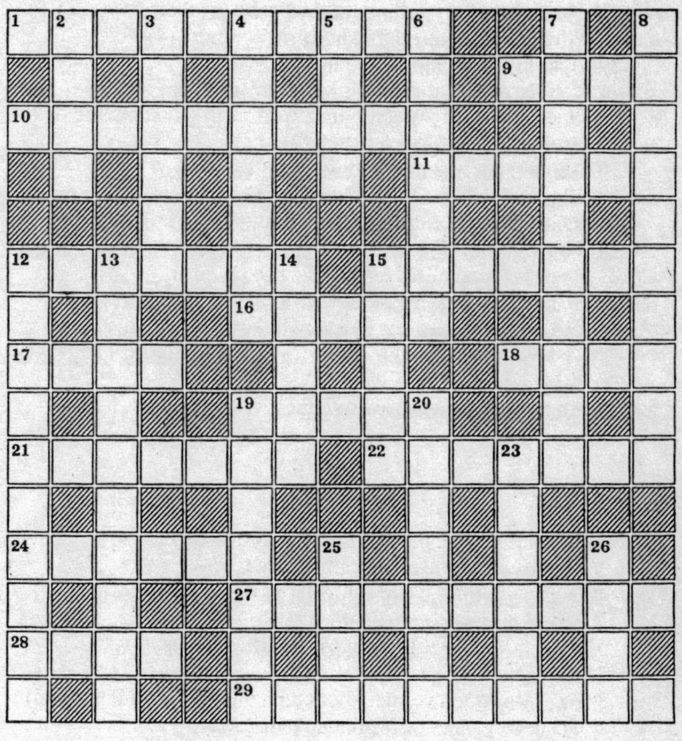

50

Across

1 Beefy team of sterling quality? (10)
6 Swing for committed murder (4)
9 Just fish at the corner of the square (5, 5)
10 I go in to bat, with the idea of hooking (4)
13 Asked in before 6 PM once (7)
15 He dictates in nasty ranting tones (6)
16 He will tell one how to back a gravel truck (6)
17 Once mixed up with evil force I'm likely to commit it (5, 2, 8)
18 One who will do sketchy work in return for it? (6)
20 Widespread dominion represented by a member of the Dail? (6)
21 Plain as back to front with an ending in reverse (7)
22 An aquatic entry the vice squad keeps an eye on (4)
25 All-round quality of enemy agent I thrice reformed inside (10)
26 Get up a wage demand? (4)
27 Angry editor out to prove he had edited, apparently (7, 3)

Down

1 No dam of 26 (4)
2 Aids for multiple construction of wood cabins (4)
3 Limit camping no longer (6)
4 Touchy journals printed for positive results (9, 6)
5 Sweetly melodious number for two which includes two numbers (6)
7 A writer producing heavy reading? (4-6)
8 Ever wet? All quite otherwise is a rainy year's problem (5-5)
11 Hackneyed amendment clause, one concerned with Australian cattle (5-5)
12 Capital ideas (10)
13 A Stainer composition, sorrowfully expressive (2, 5)
14 Evidence of some degree? (7)
19 Anything but dry bread (6)
20 The whole Northern Territory displacing the member in 20 across (6)
23 Nothing under cover for Venetian sun-worshippers (4)
24 Hindu peasant rebuilt Troy (4)

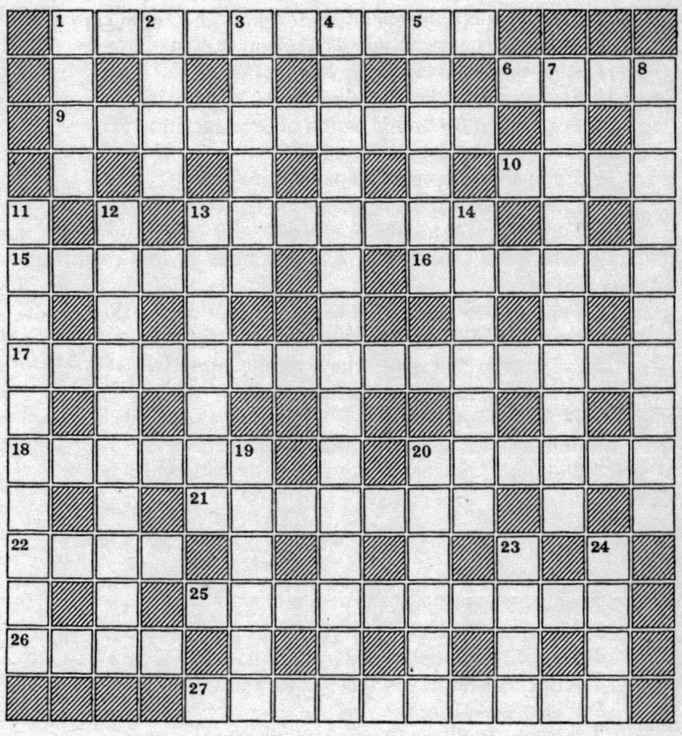

51

Across

1 Gambling conspiracy bosses for the high jump! (11)
8 Man's parliament suggests a prison (5, 2, 4)
11 Rifle workman could turn to use (4)
12 Street with the archaic eyesore (4)
13 I called out for an indication of pronunciation (7)
15 Diary MP revised in Egypt (7)
16 Rulings of shipping companies? (5)
17 Ladders looked for by batsmen (4)
18 Family is able to take in fifty (4)
19 Where from the Middle East hundreds go to a pilgrimage (6)
21 Famous racing motorist came first, but not on this kind of road where . . . (7)
22 . . . burst car tire would have resulted in such . . . (7)
23 . . . curves and smashed cars (4)
26 Blow on foot (4)
27 Sold as a lot of careless pedestrians? (7, 4)
28 Old table lights made out of brandy bottles? (6-5)

Down

2 Novel background? (4)
3 After this month everything will be put in place (7)
4 Not evil but empty deity (4)
5 NE Yorks resort? No, N Sea for them (7)
6 Radioactive fish, perhaps (4)
7 His job involves sorting out current problems (11)
8 Checking a symptom of lumbago (7, 4)
9 Excitement there is in copying the twentieth letter (11)
10 It will be cut by a couple at breakfast (7-4)
14 Gave vent to anger in publicity (5)
15 It sounds like a bit of quiet (5)
19 One who threatens mankind with race disturbance (7)
20 Blissful country song about a real bounder (7)
24 Game played off the cuff (4)
25 Poetic or down-to-earth measures (4)
26 Exchange returning prisoners-of-war (4)

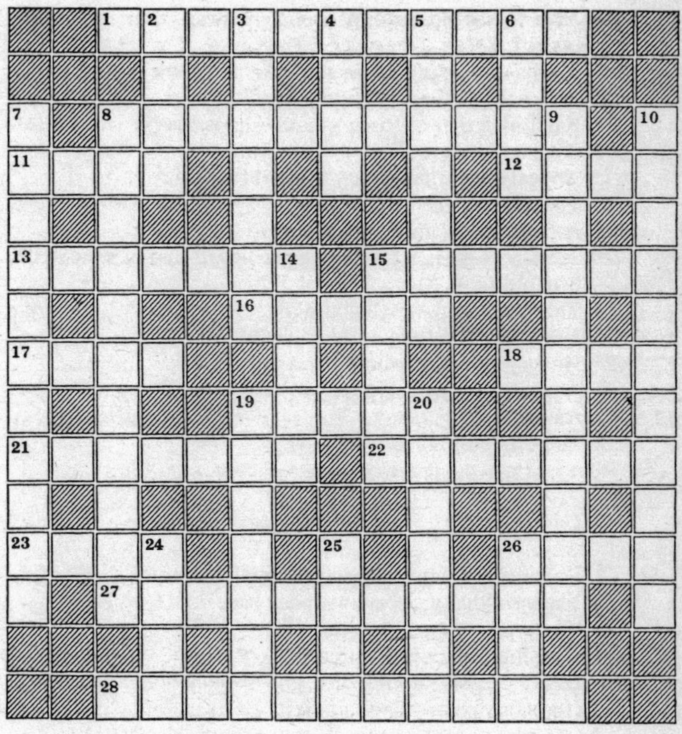

52

Across

8 Able to see things dispassionately away from the neighbours? (8)
9 A lime squash set before a Thackeray heoine (6)
10 Oriental sash 50 per cent too big (3)
11 Fighting father of Rome's trans-Alpine foe (8)
12 Badly riled about East German songs (6)
13 Appeal for parliamentary support (8, 7)
15 The clippings dad circles (7)
18 A battle study put to the proof (7)
21 Scotland's greatest swimming prodigy, if rumours are to be believed (4, 4, 7)
24 The finishing-post at Tyburn (6)
25 A woman who follows the game (8)
26 Hungry man at Plymouth? (3)
27 A Mediterranean ship on which one may enjoy a lengthy rest (6)
28 The derivation of any crest (8)

Down

1 I subsequently turn out to be a small trader (6)
2 The meal that gives mother back hard cash (6)
3 Electrical storms or worse, perhaps! (8, 7)
4 Very fond of a party with a wry grin (7)
5 Didn't achieve striking success at the junction? (6, 2, 7)
6 Humanity regards it as a pest in the main (5-3)
7 Complaints that give comfort in a Norfolk town (8)
14 Merry-hearted sin (3)
16 A niggard holding to a spray-gun, maybe (8)
17 Not how the nudist occupies himself? (8)
19 What one must do to live, even in the attic (3)
20 Confiscate the case for a change (7)
22 Italy's major lake resort (6)
23 Bring about a certain result? (6)

52

53

Across

1 And so, they lived happily in the fairy tale (4, 5)
8 The plot in which silver bells, cockle shells, and pretty maids are all lined up? (7, 6)
11 Arrange succession of command (5)
12 That place for the sappers (5)
13 Alternatively about the alternative (5)
16 Andrew is disposed to ramble (6)
17 Short measures before last month's affront (6)
18 A backward clown not joining in (5)
19 Perhaps 15 returned to obtain a bit of gold (6)
20 Cavalryman who might cut a singular figure in the quadrille (6)
21 From the Spanish south, that is her name (5)
24 Light-weight, keen-eyed, fur bearer (5)
26 Money commonly holds little gratitude for a big race representative (5)
27 Sheer off, and 17 the artist (3, 3, 7)
28 Quietly booked and kept from harm (9)

Down

2 A guard to face (5)
3 Superlatively exceptional gunners remain (6)
4 Think of a number before ten? (6)
5 Complicated welcome for a fine flyer (5)
6 Infant prodigy who should do well in 8 (7, 6)
7 The craft of customs that can reduce State income? (7-6)
9 The outlook for the Archers, perhaps (3-6)
10 Fruit drink of the gods in the Orient (9)
13 Hold forth at zero speed (5)
14 Hops round circle making more circles (5)
15 To search and rob it may produce a report (5)
22 Makes comparisons to approve on points (6)
23 Maybe a statement made by a double agent to do damage (6)
25 Come in to put on record (5)
26 Timely verbal form under stress (5)

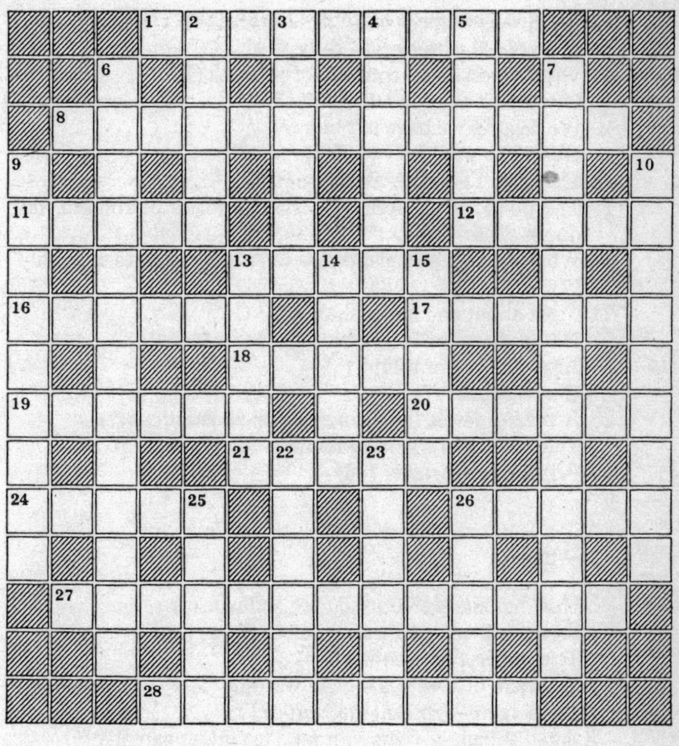

54

Across

1 It's always prudent to do this oneself! (6)
4 A shepherd with clerical duties? (6)
10 The greatest space traveller of them all (7)
11 Go too far as an invader? (7)
12 We lie after we have left him (3)
13 Dances to wind up with? (5)
14 The thread I went crazy about (5)
15 The public Shakespeare's contemporaries patronised, no doubt (7, 6)
18 What the phrenologist does even if his car rides smoothly (5, 3, 5)
23 I cast about and had a shot (5)
25 Half-a-dozen with transport for 4 (5)
26 Are rebuffed for a time (3)
27 Chops sticks? (7)
28 A wizard device for security during hostilities? (7)
29 The whole being somewhat indolent, it yields (6)
30 Permissive character? (6)

Down

1 Hurt among twelve good men and true (6)
2 As unrivalled as 10 was in pagan Rome (7)
3 Tries diverse ceremonies (5)
5 Ready to deal with a danger warning (5)
6 Not a regular entrant at Cruft's? (7)
7 Small stream or river without a tenant, apparently (6)
8 What Gulliver aroused when he arrived in Lilliput (5, 8)
9 Stroking one's way along swimmingly, like Uriah Heep maybe (5, 3, 5)
16 Old English port, not Scotch (3)
17 Wood production of 12 plus 999 (3)
19 I'd put in what happened, that's obvious (7)
20 Measure the distance by feet (4, 3)
21 The soul of a butterfly (6)
22 A middleman without funds, right? (6)
24 It may get knocked off course (5)

54

25 Never rattled, he foresaw marvellous developments in science (5)

Across

5 Perhaps the manager of 31 will go into the figure exactly (6)
8 One who won't stand for any nonsense at the meeting? (8)
9 Stable diet for the Scots (7)
10 Prose composition the trainee must learn (5)
11 Concerning a drawer that withdraws (9)
13 Residence sound as a bell with water supply installed (8)
14 What the HP firm may refuse to believe (6)
17 Norm turns tap (3)
19 Food and drink (3)
20 Councillor taking rest to fold (6)
23 Cutting jade can't be next (8)
26 Does it create minute differences in provincial drinking habits? (5, 4)
28 Best possible statement from one who holds all the cards (5)
29 Indeed let improper words be so treated (7)
30 Stayed proudly on one's own two feet? (8)
31 Property of an Eastern nation (6)

Down

1 Airmen turn red, though possibly white! (6)
2 Spotted religious scholar making the same mistake as Adam (7)
3 Sportsmen heading for a fall (9)
4 Hollow cry of warning to the Navy (6)
5 Competition for somewhere to live in Derby for instance (4-4)
6 Funny but undemanding reading matter (5)
7 Speaker on Hera's rival noted performance (8)
12 I, for example, with nothing completed (3)
15 Blow current reminders of debts and you will get more than greedy (9)
16 Rewritten titles or poems (8)
18 These eat stew. His taste is more refined (8)
21 An eccentric device on which students may have a row (3)
22 Leaves, but no grass to be found on them (7)
24 Many a precaution against the danger of short, short supply (6)

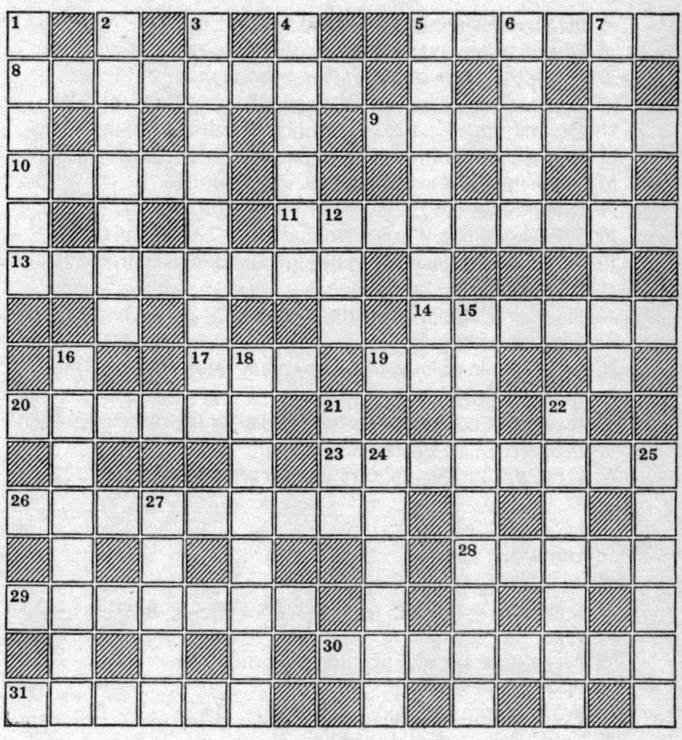

25 Blade with tooled design (6)
27 In which Christians were lionised, so to speak (5)

56

Across

1 Headgear somewhat suited to the environment (7)
5 Military convoys supplied by the press gangs? (7)
9 Pro speech chosen rightly for glowing quality (15)
10 Poems from Icelandic language otherwise dead (4)
11 Passing through it may require only a few hand-shakes (5)
12 Is in the current top ten, maybe (4)
15 Peep-hole for men of intelligence (3, 4)
16 Elderly lady who urges one to take a gamble (7)
17 Where one might expect to find either beer or spirits (7)
19 At an inquest he wants nothing hidden in the corner (7)
21 It is made in a churn (4)
22 A bed in France, but without a light (5)
23 Ain't as it should be (4)
26 What the keen buyer anticipates at (and after) the motor sale? (7, 1, 7)
27 If that pretty number is, you had better try ringing another (7)
28 Put down instruction on suit returned to the cleaner's? (7)

Down

1 Unlucky chap has presumably lost everything but his head (7)
2 More or less revealing a local accent (7, 8)
3 Record finish? (4)
4 Warning sound common in London (7)
5 Split apart, but held together (7)
6 Beat fifty-one (4)
7 Making better progress with darning a single hole? (7, 4, 4)
8 Jacket for a philosophical writer (7)
13 Animal which is a male twin? (5)
14 Horde from the South West prepare for war (5)
17 Fiddle for Dee or Dum (7)
18 Took charge, but he paid the price of responsibility, it would seem (7)
19 Rose, perhaps – that was his intention? (7)
20 Reprimands for naval personnel (7)
24 Head or tail of 2 (4)

56

25 The journey no skipper wants to do (4)

57

Across

1 Essential requirement for a saluting base in Arizona (9)
9 Don's off-putting expression? (6)
10 Small rises that naturally lead to bigger ones (9)
11 She sees it differently (6)
12 The American independence fighters Gulliver came across in Lilliput (6-3)
13 A step the promising student may be urged to take (6)
17 A champion card to play? (3)
19 Second honeymoon, maybe, in which 25 played an important part! (8, 7)
20 Sturdily built water-tower (3)
21 Devils one outwardly wards off (6)
25 They were rather more than mere versifiers (4, 5)
26 Gary follows us back with cloying sweetness (6)
27 Capable of double-talk? (9)
28 Part of India or South Africa is included in it (6)
29 A tent site changed unwillingly (9)

Down

2 Casually pop round to see what's on TV (4, 2)
3 Produce a rather abrupt eviction order (3, 3)
4 Fresh detail closely followed (6)
5 A trumped-up charge of treachery? (5, 10)
6 Say good-bye to work for a while, presumably (4, 5)
7 Slap-up tomb for an old German aristocrat (9)
8 Flowery productions of a Dutch artist with the heart to revolt (9)
14 One who claims to be a top university man (9)
15 The scent of a whale (9)
16 Pickwickian fellows brought up on cattle-food (9)
17 Tiny island I put in at (3)
18 Labour measure? (3)
22 Corrupt passage (6)
23 What toughs may be – by the police? (6)
24 Ultimately working as a shoemaker? (2, 4)

57

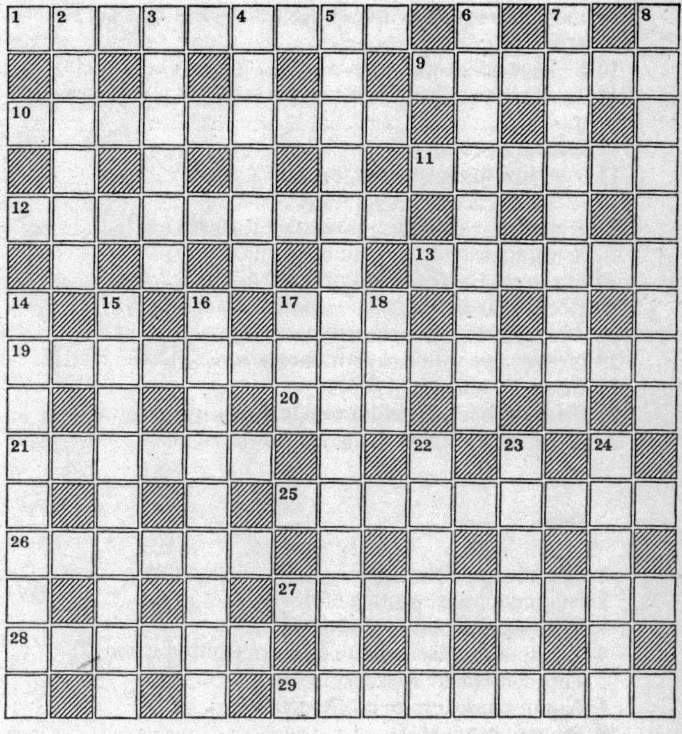

58

Across

7 and 8 Came to hail British Rail chaos and rush aid to the artist (5-4, 5)
10 Sit back on the awkward beast in 7 for traveller's joy (8)
11 The French military unit reorganised for a foreign seaman (6)
12 Restful places in polar regions (4)
13 I am free to move? No! (8)
16 Observe a Scottish river in turbulence (4)
18 Plan to give diminutive Diana a bit of weight (7)
20 What gin can be doing to break the ice? (7)
22 She loved Narcissus, it is recalled (4)
24 One and 28 in time become a devout admirer (8)
26 Absorbed in a complicated part (4)
29 Namely one with a royal monogram in a Moslem land (6)
30 Count of 4, German style (8)
31 Slave of the ambassador to fate (5)
32 Early variety found oddly in own teapot (3, 6)

Down

1 Idle note to a friend (5)
2 Is he confined to writing? (6)
3 Resolved with ease in the main (5, 3)
4 Transporter of songs with a cheering introduction (7)
5 They once made a bolt for it (8)
6 As canvas worker he is offensive (9)
9 Bridge closure? (4)
14 Traditional concept in the Ptolemy theory (4)
15 Charming but ratty player who did not get his due (4, 5)
17 A winger from the Middle-East in the Home Counties (4)
19 Sounds just the vessel for a ship's cook (8)
21 It once led sailors a merry dance (8)
23 Public announcer holds little weight for the bishop's staff (7)
25 Was it subject to inflation when Alexander took over? (4)
27 Much outpouring from the cornucopia (6)
28 Same again for one non-drinker in the party (5)

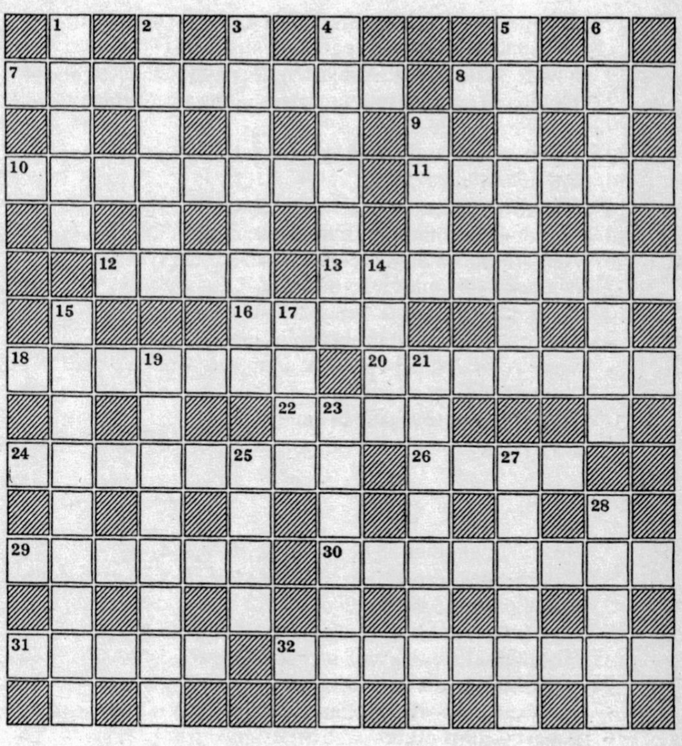

Across

1 The first quip of the day . . . (5, 2, 4)
8 . . . appertaining to its period of decline? (11)
11 Said to indicate favourable conditions over the Atlantic (4)
12 Uninteresting character in *Love's Labour's Lost* (4)
13 Topside cooked in earnest (7)
15 Artist in a part of London that's far from monotonous (7)
16 Specific callings (5)
17 Page with margin precisely as it should be? (4)
18 Fabulous brother in sombre raiment (4)
19 A sportsman who is encouraged to strike (5)
21 Managed to continue in Burma (7)
22 Helped to descend to betrayal? (3, 4)
23 They man the warships he whips out (4)
26 They are very much like wild apes (4)
27 Young ladies of class (11)
28 Highly prosperous part of Europe (11)

Down

2 Rex takes another boy out – an Irish one (4)
3 and 19 down Yorkshire skipper who had an unfriendly reception in Co. Mayo (7, 7)
4 Empty-headed fool climbing a peak in Thessaly (4)
5 He makes do with a slug of a sort (7)
6 Early British military decoration (4)
7 The exuberant vivacity for which Speyside is famous (4, 7)
8 A gin cocktail swallowed by the tented troops (11)
9 Basic requirements for a quiet walk? (6, 5)
10 Blooming extravagance on the part of the author (11)
14 Feature of a bird of prey a pound in weight (5)
15 Brew of beer left to rise, maybe (5)
19 See 3
20 Result of a successful appeal, perhaps (7)
24 Dutch boat company in Cornwall? (4)
25 A song to take part in (4)
26 Constructive idea (4)

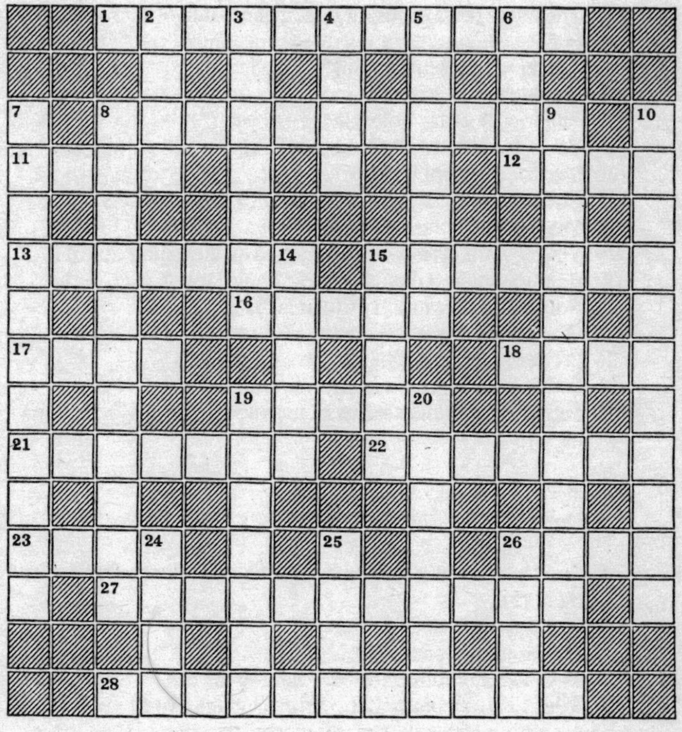

60

Across

1 The latest news on using pedestrian-controlled crossings? (4-5)
8 Agreeing to attend school? (6, 2, 5)
11 Workers on watch (5)
12 The first singular object is the subject (5)
13 Town from which Arabs come? (5)
16 Size for a school book (6)
17 Code letter giving you something to chew over (6)
18 Tree found in bare canyons (5)
19 Yet they are often worn by gymnasts loosening up (6)
20 Beggars do, and dirty beggars should, too (6)
21 Foot often takes such measures (5)
24 Hit the nail (5)
26 Perhaps it gives details of the next race (5)
27 Led by two fools, one state's drastic solution? (13)
28 Father returns platter anew, for another helping of it, perhaps (5-4)

Down

2 Tear into street which is up, and you'll probably suffer them (5)
3 Building for a deity in Pennsylvania (6)
4 He has a top construction job (6)
5 Two pages required for bed-making (5)
6 Additional accommodation for the bank? (8-5)
7 Assuming different character, the great one was Oppenheim's novel effort (13)
9 Eating utensil for meat on credit (9)
10 Alloy for producing the best rings (4-5)
13 Metal type of band, maybe (5)
14 Vegetable from Scandinavia (5)
15 Collect could be used in it (5)
22 Organ weights over one pound (6)
23 Small basket put about $22\frac{1}{2}^\circ$ (6)
25 A vagrant sometimes harboured (5)
26 The poet's always about at one to take in food (5)

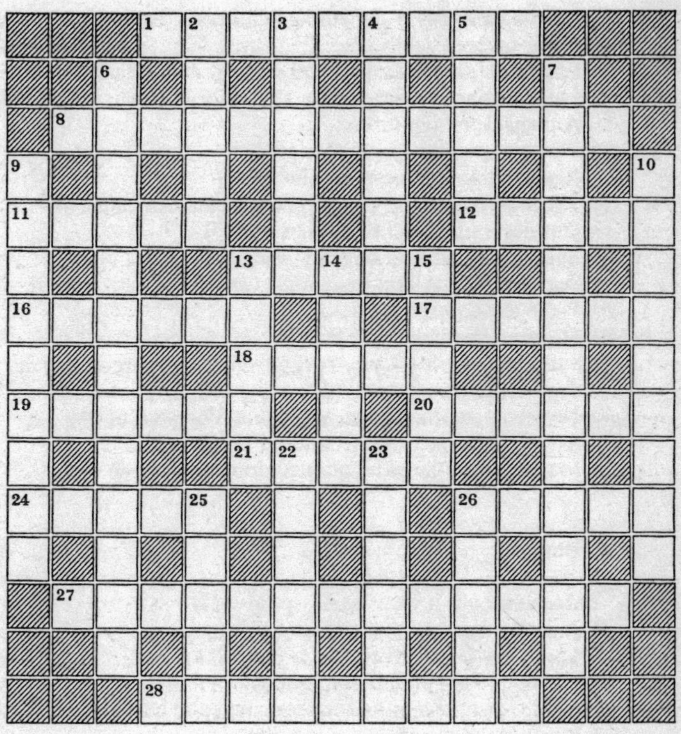
1
2
3
4
5
6
7
8
9
10
11
12
13
14
15
16
17
18
19
20
21
22
23
24
25
26
27
28

61

Across

1 Bowling analysis is something of an exaggeration (13)
10 Killer races in wildly (7)
11 Essayist of the underworld taken in by a fellow (7)
12 Later, but not too late (2, 4)
15 A pinnacle to aim for (6)
16 Waste of petrol and tire (7)
17 Real trouble for one who is belted (4)
18 The most frequently broken components of a clutch (4)
19 One decoration said to be depraved (7)
20 Baste food that may be hard (4)
22 Seaweed from Albert to Georgia (4)
24 Piano left covered by sack (7)
26 Stumble, lose head, and fall (6)
27 Suffering the lot from party having overthrown small demonstration (6)
30 No secretive demeanour, not within four walls (4-3)
31 An inter-change to get from road to rail? (7)
32 Maybe where the radio or television is kept (9–4)

Down

2 One who calls it wearing a face-saver (7)
3 Are men disposed to give a new title (6)
4 Credit lost by the pawner of a watch? (4)
5 It is not all up, even if one is caught in it (4)
6 After a manner a pious man is expected to be (6)
7 Preparing to brood, mixed ten gins (7)
8 Appearance of famine units waiting to 31? (13)
9 Sympathetic though not above putting both feet down (13)
13 Formerly sufficient for instance (7)
14 Loud colours, presumably (7)
15 Not proud of a primitive dwelling in which mother was raised (7)
21 Contend for favourite income (7)
23 Subject for patient back-chat (7)
24 A polite utterance will (6)
25 Order list (6)
28 Child who could become a little baronet (4)

61

29 A fighter in the past, now a mere cipher (4)

62

Across

1 How one may arrive at a sounder judgement? Yes and no! (2, 10)
8 Not many are disposed to define what is good to bad (7)
9 A cushion put away in Cornwall (7)
11 Work interrupted by a sort of rum commotion (7)
12 Think of your safety but don't be introspective (4, 3)
13 What pigeons will seek after a race round the Orkneys and Shetlands? (5)
14 Go into a place after fish and chips, maybe! (9)
16 A blow we don't want when there's a freeze (9)
19 Salubrious bathing resort (5)
21 An African state, and it could be a large one (7)
23 Completely cleared of the charge (7)
24 One doesn't lightly ask to do so (7)
25 Pretentious building (7)
26 The last word in radio sets when they first came out (4-8)

Down

1 Small number up to three going round a lake in North America (7)
2 Clearly sound touring organisation (4, 3)
3 Type of private vehicle that is relatively popular (6, 3)
4 Turn out a bad scholar? (5)
5 Immature political hack of the Victorian period (7)
6 Military detachment awaiting collection? (7)
7 Unassailable argument for a strong-box (4-4, 4)
10 What one might call a marine plant that grows in pools and ditches (5-7)
15 Prosaic injunction to the overworked linesman (9)
17 Annual display of Venetian craftsmanship, for example (7)
18 Hemmed in by clucking females, a rural dean becomes callous (7)
19 Old Greek soldier I help to rehabilitate (7)
20 The servants of Fleet Street? (7)
22 When dropped from a hit, it is what you don't hear – or do! (5)

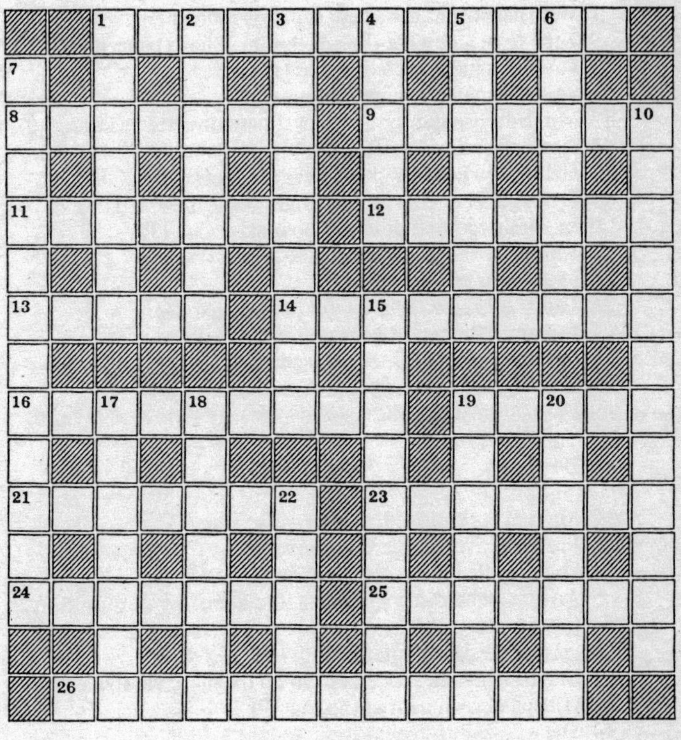

63

Across

1 With its citizens departed, is its spirit nowt changed? (5, 4)
9 Tape to secure what the poacher may have bagged (6)
10 Pavlova catalogues historians (9)
11 Suitable road for a rendezvous (6)
12 Mournfully coloured Scottish stream diverted to Lancs? (9)
13 Agreement as dispatched (6)
17 Help lass who has suffered a capital loss (3)
19 Catchy sort of chorus that might be heard in 1 (8, 7)
20 In youth you find your old possessive case (3)
21 Raised in line like a wolf (6)
25 Mere trifle of a game (9)
26 Fancy dress for the steel-worker's hearth (6)
27 Ice target broken, it goes up in smoke (9)
28 Princess is returned, burnt brown (6)
29 Fencing keeping out some of the workers (9)

Down

2 Manual control held an alternative way (6)
3 In fright, five score become rare (6)
4 She provided cover for Svengali (6)
5 An excellent defence against the elements of suspicion? (10, 5)
6 Stops as a sign of late autumn? (6, 3)
7 Maybe a match for Nell Gwyn on the march in Belfast (9)
8 Putting one on oath at the trial (9)
14 She will angle – for natives, etc? (9)
15 Hung up and temporarily debarred from office (9)
16 I train ten for travelling . . . (9)
17 . . . to which this little worker puts an end (3)
18 Desiccated condition of 5? (3)
22 Material with which the American attorney won't show his face in court? (6)
23 Desolate rat (6)
24 A plant variety that's a tree (6)

64

Across

1 Well-filled team with a wonderful notion (5, 4)
8 Top-grade soccer clubs in which offenders are leniently handled! (5, 8)
11 Narrow passage where a shout reverberates (5)
12 Chancy game many take to (5)
13 Coarse oatmeal for which the Pennines are noted (5)
16 The colourless fuel Athene transformed (6)
17 It goes to the Wash with a Frenchman (6)
18 A girl from whom one stands aloof (5)
19 Steer clumsily round a remote island (6)
20 Physical training instructor? (6)
21 Out-of-work problem? (5)
24 A sound I show curiosity about (5)
26 Goes around selling birds of prey (5)
27 He usually keeps his stock till he can sell it at a good profit (6, 7)
28 The case that can be made for a leather seat (6-3)

Down

2 Thin foreign agent from the West Indies? (5)
3 Accounts book in which the margin goes from left to right (6)
4 How an American billiards player appears to lay out his funds? (6)
5 A canvas holder, maybe (5)
6 Place specially marked for military operations (5, 8)
7 What the worker is usually expected to do (5-4, 4)
9 The girl from the pâtisserie just beyond the boulevards of Paris (9)
10 How to heat steel to make it conform to pattern? (9)
13 A kind of green (5)
14 Norwegian who created problems for the theatre (5)
15 An Indian who devotes his life to teaching (5)
22 Greek bathing beauty (6)
23 Bound to be paid for? (6)
25 Actor unlikely to get more than the usual fee (5)
26 It may produce howls of laughter (5)

64

65

Across

1 Perhaps cork could he obtained from its wood (6–4)
8 Two small boys and the one they attack (6)
9 What the usurious and careless car-battery service department may do (10)
10 Nothing if not about an expression of disgust (6)
11 Satanic scheme, perhaps, that requires spadework (6, 4)
12 Bars composed to sing (6)
13 Not up to what one may find in 11 (4)
15 The thing in a cow's nose for tying up? (7)
19 Studying at one of the universities (7)
21 Island bound in conventionalism (4)
22 With which a violinist could play a tied note? (6)
25 From now on a Scottish banker starts from here (10)
27 Criminal end of big return by a bit of gambling (6)
28 The knave, with the queen later, is enough to raise the roof (4-6)
29 Household task leads to a complaint that shakes one (6)
30 Revised opinion of fools taken in by broken reeds (10)

Down

1 It sounds cleaner than either a horse or motor vehicle (8)
2 Beneficiaries covered by last letter of credit belonging to them (6)
3 Key to the cupboard? (6)
4 Tread softly after the market rises (5)
5 Happening to die in convulsions sometime before nightfall (8)
6 Direction colonel recommended, having been beaten (8)
7 Colour acquired by the user of an ultraviolet lamp? (5, 3)
13 Past a green light? (3)
14 Time to turn over 100 square metres (3)
16 Unqualified, but not in the wrong (8)
17 Storm-petrel? No, just a woodpecker . . . (4-4)
18 . . . that gives one a shock after dark (8)
20 Got together and tucked in (8)
23 Before game footballers turn fiery (6)
24 What the author does to describe Western ceremonies (6)

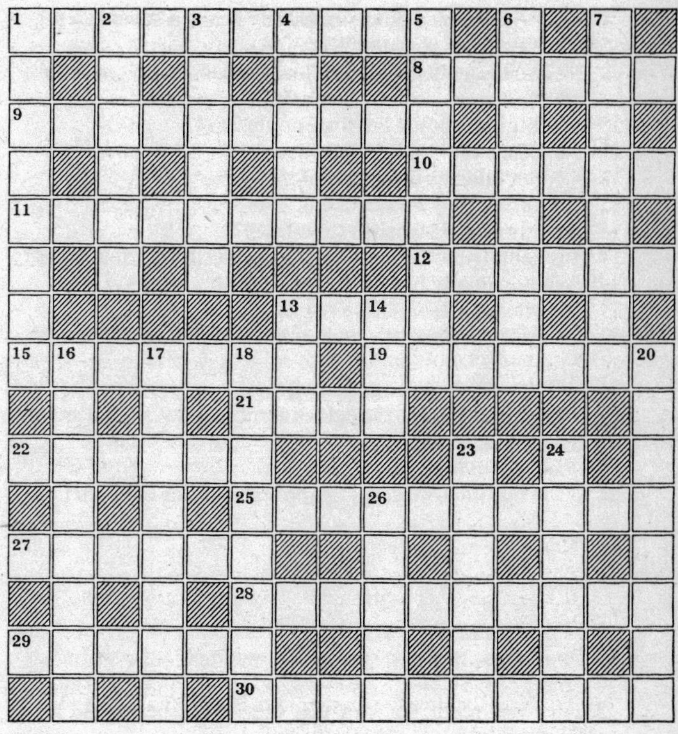

26 They could be sponges and soaps (5)

Across

1 Prices halved by a point are usually below a sovereign (7)
5 City associated with the Wash (4)
9 His skilful quality added colour to landscape gardening (10, 5)
10 Well off Frenchman is a food producer (4)
11 One being vital to the whole body (5)
12 A cutter adds by the sound of it (4)
15 The party's play on words (7)
16 Conspicious foreigner in the street (7)
17 It is kept by the master – the maths master, no doubt (3-4)
19 Fred apparently has stomach ache with scallops (7)
21 Bid when both sides have scored 100 (4)
22 An oyster without one must surely have had a close shave (5)
23 Still unsettled none married (4)
26 Game alternative to the lighter or more serious problems of crowd control (8, 7)
27 Look equal (4)
28 Witty headline, maybe, not applicable to the old yarn (3-4)

Down

1 Main area of peace (7)
2 Capacious measure to which metricationist colonials object? (8, 6)
3 They will scout the idea that they could be foxed (4)
4 Cross sailor covers anger (7)
5 Cooks but not captains may put them in to bowl? (7)
6 Underground but only up to a point (4)
7 Good community study outlet (7)
8 Puckish Robin's cheering introduction to social camaraderie (4-10)
13 Army expression of disapproval is forbidden (5)
14 Everyone accounted for at the base, even though exhausted (3, 2)
17 A match for the devil himself (7)
18 One who doesn't stand for prayer (7)
19 They give a warning of course to the work force (7)

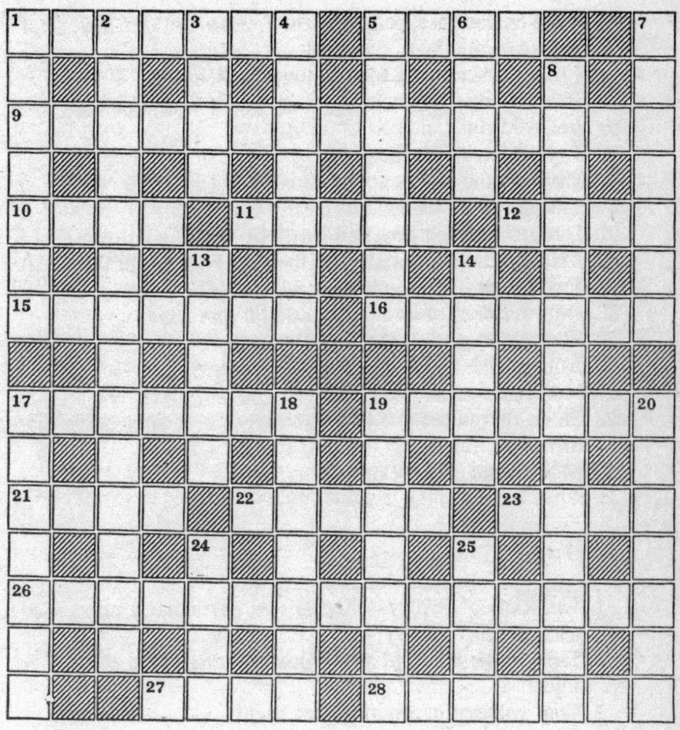

20 Odd song composed by him was called 'A-sitting On a Gate' (7)
24 Fit table without top (4)
25 Wild West dish (4)

67

Across

1 and 4 Altogether, people by the dozen are said to have slept in it (5, 3, 2, 4)
8 I ring Neddy about a spot of refreshment (5)
9 Possibly suspicious conduct in which lion and tiger are involved (9)
11 Every tea-chest losing 3 (4)
12 How are the dog's ears for sensing an early caller? (5)
13 The clothes in which one drives (4)
16 Unnatural brightness that won't be found in 4 down (8, 5)
19 Maybe a Londoner who deserves nothing but praise (7, 6)
20 Two nickels I'd brought back with me (4)
22 Old love-feast showing a wonderful reaction (5)
23 A machine-gun nest in bad shape (4)
26 Automobile agent allocated to a city in Spain (9)
27 Not exactly what the challenger sought? (5)
28 Polite thing to say if you want easy sleep, after being disturbed (3, 6)
29 Makes a final check on board (5)

Down

1 The kind of relations Euclid was particularly concerned with (9)
2 The way in which Mistress Quickly entertained Falstaff & Co (9)
3 Trial game of international status (4)
4 A blooming price-list from Holland, perhaps! (4, 9)
5 A dependency of the kingdom of Fife? (4)
6 One team that gives confidence to those watching the play (5)
7 Small boy that is climbing a difficult Alpine peak (5)
10 A tree that leans over a slope (8, 5)
14 Dee's silted estuary (5)
15 Luxuriously Lydian piece, in the manner of Christopher (5)
17 Leave behind? But one doesn't have to (2, 7)
18 What bank-robbers do during, and detectives after, the raid (4, 5)
20 False front that's decidedly shaky (5)

21 Means of identifying foreign currency (5)
24 Deal roughly with a wood beetle? (4)
25 I am upset, monsieur, and badly hurt (4)

68

Across

1 Enough to cause a gentle roll at sea, which is fortunate (4, 2, 4)
9 Gilbertian official repeatedly floored? (2-2)
10 Happened to arrive at a narrow defile (4, 2, 4)
11 Beheaded another and scrambled for a fine seat (6)
12 Serving man round the Pole is no sluggard (7)
15 Tower of strength (7)
16 Commonly understand it could be on foot (5)
17 Capital support, often collared (4)
18 Means of storing blended oils (4)
19 Church member entrance (5)
21 Give voice to an evil complaint (4, 3)
22 Somehow it's fit for a literary family name (7)
24 Right tree-shoot looking more hopeful (6)
27 Stood between the artist and his model? (10)
28 Types including socially acceptable birds (4)
29 Could Naomi have acted thus without her favourite daughter-in-law? (10)

Down

2 Fabulous tree from America, around Philadelphia (4)
3 He is an abstainer embracing a believer (6)
4 Located in a measly condition? (7)
5 Dash out of the hotel annexe (4)
6 Endure the French drink (4, 3)
7 Engineering product of America's crazy desire (10)
8 Genuine hard work – to the lions, anyhow (6, 4)
12 The way of 007? (4, 6)
13 Order suggesting ringside helpers are poor timekeepers (7, 3)
14 Just a word of agreement (5)
15 Rows a little river in knots (5)
19 He rubs down and dresses after a tanning (7)
20 Violent blow in the Rhône valley (7)
23 Exultant expressions of TV doctor over minor operations (6)
25 Printing instruction of note in a small way (4)

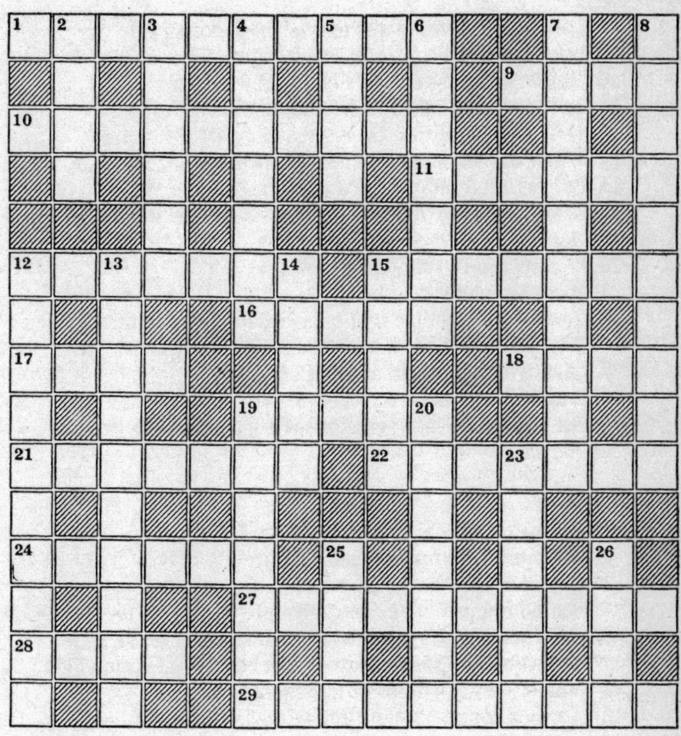

26 Cruel hill (4)

69

Across

1 Large-scale investments to control imports? (9)
9 Long time without aural sex literature (7)
10 Quarrels that blow over (7)
11 Tell too many untruths to smother, maybe (7)
12 That Teeswater bull Odin's son cut out? (9)
14 Water barrier in a town near Manchester (5, 3)
15 Bands that fight or retreat amid peaks (6)
17 Knock a couple of fifties, then a duck, on the Italian Riviera (7)
20 In a position to shoot? (6)
23 Show I can edit afresh (8)
25 Commercial gamble that offers exciting possibilities? (9)
26 One who has made his mark as a pugilist (7)
27 Gives young Donald a setback (7)
28 Rather less than 50 per cent (3, 4)
29 Put together a catalogue for the 16, perhaps (9)

Down

2 Cross-bred animal that can't go straight? (7)
3 Casual leave (7)
4 Heart-broken West country nymph (8)
5 and 6 Romantic revival over in an instant? (6, 9)
7 Girl who gives short measure to a boy from Scotland (7)
8 What Essen can do to be intelligible (4, 5)
13 Stormed round Virginia and wrought havoc (7)
15 Armed citizens instrumental in bringing harmony to B R? (5-4)
16 A stickler for details? Exactly! (9)
18 Inspired utterance of a linesman who has lost heart, presumably (4, 4)
19 Will take some small change, apparently (7)
21 Is least disposed to weigh anchor (3, 4)
22 Birds that dive for little fishes in America (7)
24 Moroccan tribesman doing home defence duty? (6)

69

Across

1 Residence for one ordained many years after (8)
5 Escort arranged for Spanish adventurer (6)
9 Joey making progress by leaps and bounds (8)
10 Leader of the funeral procession (6)
11 Score but one (8)
13 Tried to catch up with some decoration? (6)
14 Strange spirit (3)
16 When one is most likely to find an adder (6)
19 Two requirements for tennis game (7)
20 Weeps about many sins (6)
21 Doubtless he made the leather sizzle off the bat (3)
26 Tiring walks? (6)
27 It would be ridden only in a main event presumably (3-5)
28 Accustomed to ruined ruin (6)
29 They go on foot, though are clearly not sure-footed (8)
30 Well-oiled little Greek midshipman (6)
31 One who irregularly rewins about 500-pound (8)

Down

1 Old Scandinavian ruler under six (6)
2 Is it possible for gin sling to be regarded as punishment? (6)
3 One withdrawn from reality finds an interest in landed property (6)
4 Glare from a cigarette in the dark? (6)
6 Pass a complete renovation (8)
7 Tedious rise wrongly entered in the big book (8)
8 They don't save by betting on those that finish (8)
12 Biblical census figures (7)
15 Is it a Dartmoor tor? Certainly (3)
16 Christopher Wily (3)
17 Airmen upset over article will be highly critical (8)
18 With trigonometrical formula the remedy is an easy job (8)
19 Goods with a point that's quite unnecessary (8)
22 Colourful description of cowards who cry out in pain (6)
23 Did he compose his work or just jaw about it? (6)
24 Alternative harbour trial (6)
25 Landl..d (6)

71

Across

8 Gaul troubled by deep sleep that interferes with vision (8)
9 From the Tiber I admire Spain and Portugal (6)
10 For a reason that's childish but still gives one the angle (3)
11 Descriptive of one conversant with the source of literature (4-4)
12 I get on somehow, though lacking the line for conforming (6)
13 At which momentous forces are balanced with never a crack? (6, 2, 7)
15 Guards with faces covered by hands (7)
18 Tales that may have a lift to them (7)
21 It quite literally taxes one's honesty (10, 5)
24 Maybe diamond in one or two of a kind 6)
25 Not turning down flat application for general exhibition certificate? (2-6)
26 Drink half of . . . (3)
27 . . . a lager brew that's as sour as vinegar (6)
28 Terse American backing given to county council in Connecticut (8)

Down

1 Declare understanding member in 26 (6)
2 Count up backwards to find a new layer (6)
3 Only heir who doesn't belong to the upper class? (4, 11)
4 He was told to lay on some dough protected from the rain (7)
5 Cheap tubes tried out to create a riot (7, 3, 5)
6 Set to be a criminal accomplice (8)
7 Portrait in which six get mixed up with ten (8)
14 Negative (3)
16 Description of a top dog in particular (5, 3)
17 The actors get mixed gins supplied by the founder (8)
19 The final particle in electrolytic action (3)
20 In search of a means of establishing the cause of death (7)
22 Ring up doctor with own Scotch to prescribe (6)
23 The girl from the East, refined and fastidious (6)

71

Across

1 Rebuilt phaetons in which no passengers could be taken for a drive (8)
5 A hint now pointless, apparently (3-3)
9 A through carriageway? (8)
10 Request fresh air for an East African militant (6)
11 The only way the coaster can go? (8)
12 Underclothes of little character (6)
14 Sharply picked out (3-7)
18 How the old doctor stuck to his patients? (4, 1, 5)
22 The hold we had against the French at the time of Napoleon (6)
23 Settle the bill for justice to press suit? (3, 5)
24 A flower plucked out of the Tiber, I suppose, or . . . (6)
25 . . . one that sounds a disconsolate warning, perhaps (8)
26 He's after expansive fuel cuts (6)
27 Smiles exchanged with an inhabitant of the Hebrides (8)

Down

1 Come away from a party? (6)
2 New wars or old weapons (6)
3 A position of some eminence (6)
4 Made an official announcement in favour of decimal conversion (10)
6 One can't sleep through it (8)
7 Easily the most convenient way to collect church funds? (2, 1, 5)
8 The reverse of a hit in the pop world (4-4)
13 Sights that come in pairs (10)
15 Monarch of the glens rattling his chains? (8)
16 Groups about to do away with kitchen utensils (8)
17 Stream of traffic interrupted by a cipher girl (8)
19 Agree to submit the small bill first (6)
20 A show-place of antiquity perhaps (6)
21 Dictator whose memory has not been left without blemish! (6)

72

73

Across

1 In a state once mentioned as an example (7)
5 Good-bye and thanks, thanks again (2-2)
9 March may be said to make a powerful entry (4, 2, 4, 1, 4)
10 Plan a piece of ground (4)
11 A set of round dots placed in an upright position (5)
12 A post-war celebratory day to ban (4)
15 Yet little Edward is calmed (7)
16 Hopeless condition of the milkmaid in Jack's DIY home (7)
17 You alone in wit art lacking (7)
19 Constraint of the 007 era (7)
21 A joker, no doubt? (4)
22 Maybe a handy bit of advice on 10 (5)
23 The priest's charge for an effective remedy (4)
26 In the main, an inclination to the right (4, 2, 9)
27 Become somewhat ragged a conflict (4)
28 Put off by dyed ale concoction (7)

Down

1 As safety equipment, they are good when successfully made (7)
2 Ten metric moons assembled for mutual advantage (6, 8)
3 Excursion resulting from not watching one's step (4)
4 Struck out hindrance indeed (7)
5 Mimicry that's no come-down (4-3)
6 Gin on wheels (4)
7 Enfeebled and disparaged (3, 4)
8 Extensive verbal choice, broadly speaking? (4, 10)
13 Everyone to return and share out (5)
14 Elephantine pick-up for luggage (5)
17 Where the light presumably won't last long in Ireland (7)
18 Dry? Try this mixture (7)
19 Ship and freebooter (7)
20 Direction restored and text corrected (7)
24 Common prison agitation (4)
25 An early victim from Elba (4)

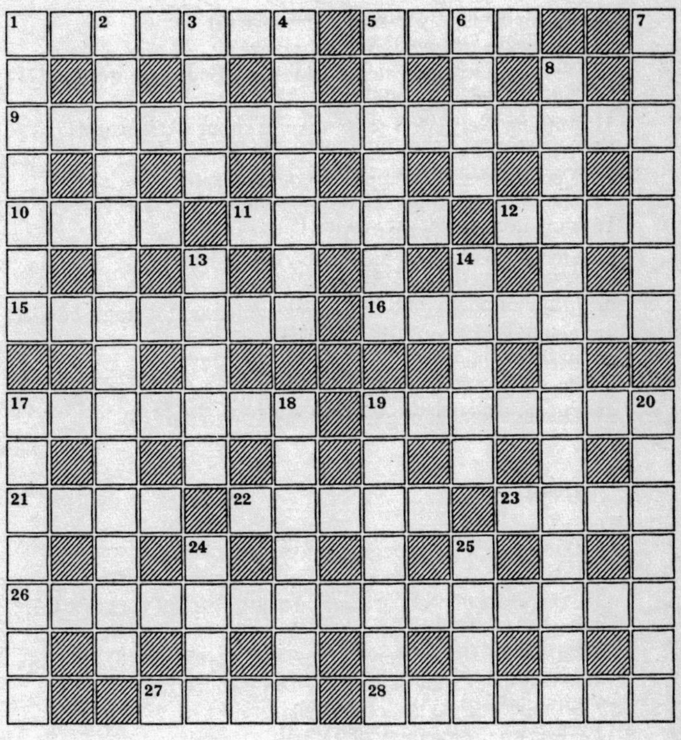

Across

5 Remarkable way to send a message (6)
8 Go away empty? (5, 3)
9 American world-beater embraced by English flower girl (7)
10 A timber man quietly installed (5)
11 Making every effort to be waspish about wet weather (9)
13 What I did at the restaurant to get started (8)
14 Keeps down the number of boundaries (6)
17 Nigerian tribesman who rejects witchcraft (3)
19 Elegant female writer (3)
20 Unable to carry on indefinitely (6)
23 Not simple to make up (8)
26 Some Chinese propaganda to brighten up the home? (9)
28 Arguments put forward for boxes (5)
29 Beefeaters working as invoice clerks? (7)
30 Go on and knock someone down, maybe (4, 4)
31 Documents that ought to be right up to date (6)

Down

1 Lunchtime bills brought up for sea-food (6)
2 From a spider Bruce learned how to conquer it (7)
3 Composite of peculiar merit in a large part of the globe (9)
4 Pernickety language master (6)
5 Variety of 18 that may be kept in a warehouse (8)
6 A very small unit of artillery-men trapped (5)
7 Stranger tucked in to spoil relations (8)
12 Clear up the meaning of X (3)
15 Awkwardly situated but assured of preservation? (2, 1, 6)
16 A salmon I made a fine picture of (4, 4)
18 About fifty craftsmen from Yarmouth? (8)
21 A pip of a service! (3)
22 Dogs I have running with the 19 (7)
24 He is eloquent with an appeal to 25 or . . . (6)
25 . . . waste (6)
27 The French city two apprentices give false information about (5)

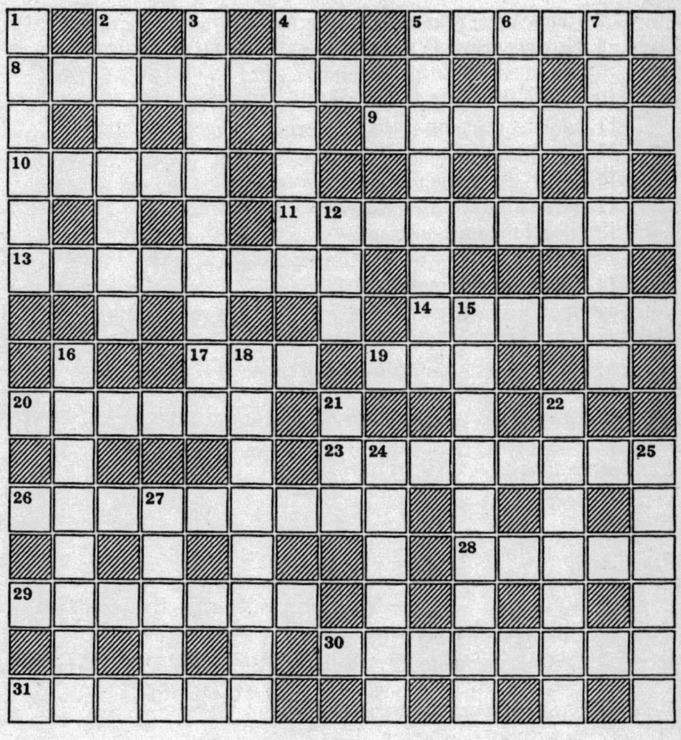

75

Across

1 Choose the French preserve (6)
4 Local levy breaks creditor – making a bit of a hole in things (6)
10 Bridge that could give one quite a turn (7)
11 Journalist's terse self-announcement, and what he hopes it will do? (7)
12 Have won somehow (3)
13 Their move to somewhere to Kent (5)
14 Royal Highlanders take one valley in France (5)
15 They figure a great deal in official surveys (13)
18 Touching spectacles? (7, 6)
23 That part of the boot that could supply meals amidships (5)
25 Fresh pleas become invalid in time (5)
26 Eggs not altogether oval (3)
27 In all justice he should win everything except the bride (4, 3)
28 Gregory XIII introduced it as a time for resolution (3, 4)
29 Constraint socially acceptable in habit (6)
30 Joints near to hand (6)

Down

1 Bill the mail clerk? (6)
2 Old vehicle for modern version of the Boston Tea Party (7)
3 Launch without a business-expense meal? (5)
5 Australian river cowboy? (5)
6 Maybe bound 12 to keep from moving (3, 4)
7 First showings of shots from a film about Moses? (6)
8 Perhaps they give sideways looks at their exasperating sergeants! (5-8)
9 East Indian grower providing a natural target for Don Quixote (8-5)
16 First class Northern version of 12 (3)
17 Beast has removed page from the passage (3)
19 He doesn't support work on the model (7)
20 Talk non-stop? (7)
21 Checked the dog-basket maybe (6)
22 Suit beaters (6)

75

24 Early Roman, like his brother (5)
25 Frown, but being not so uppish? (5)

76

Across

1 Professional man who goes to work on foot (11)
9 Most important part of architecture (4)
10 Alternative to the lighter and more romantic kind of marriage? (6-5)
11 It could be used to make a ring, friend (4)
14 Pipe 19 aboard (7)
16 Rests, but not when it comes to further modelling (7)
17 Perhaps he told father about how many stones he took and slung (5)
18 Dandy's pointed walking-stick? (4)
19 High up at work (4)
20 Bar for purchase (5)
22 Given a light form of dieting (7)
23 Deserter's retreat? (3-4)
24 Music that goes with a swing till composed (4)
28 Invaluable pot in the kitchen has made a capital investment, but . . . (11)
29 . . . with old copper one is swindled (4)
30 Cords for roping carrier held by 28 perhaps (6, 5)

Down

2 Make hale (4)
3 Dance one may get a line on (4)
4 Keep supplying timber, laminated type (7)
5 Dull sailor under the doctor (4)
6 Withdrew with South East handed over to the enemy (7)
7 In favour of job suggestion (11)
8 His poor help confused a man of wisdom (11)
12 Wine waiter's complaint that he must work right up to the year dot? (11)
13 What Darwin sought under his dressing-table (7, 4)
15 Father showed the way, but grew nervous? (5)
16 Cam, for instance, that splits open (5)
20 One left something – something to stand on – something to stand a ball on (7)
21 American farmer ran about with her (7)
25 Mark of battle in which Wilde loses his head (4)

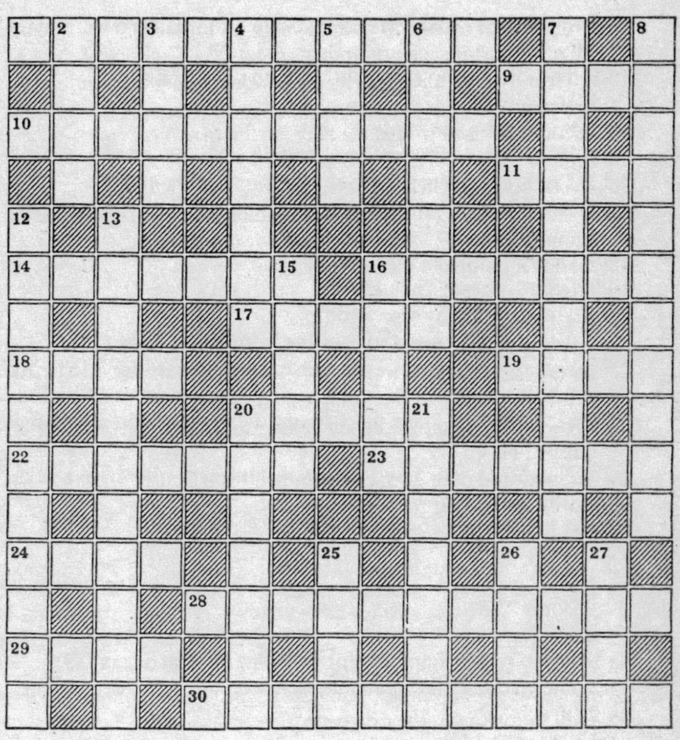

26 A famous orchestra too (4)
27 Make one's way from the West End (4)

Across

1 and 4 Use bulldozers to evacuate a football crowd, maybe (5, 3, 6)
8 The Phoenician trade outlet Pluto turned on (5)
9 High-minded? (9)
11 Spot cash abroad (4)
12 Have a go at literary composition (5)
13 The first emperor the Germans had to turn to (4)
16 Indubitably the best young delinquents are in this permissive day and age! (3, 2, 2, 6)
19 Deceptive skill (7-2-4)
20 Poet over one's head? (4)
22 The craft Cathy wrecked (5)
23 Admiral who was shot not far from New Guinea (4)
26 Expensive portion of meat is apparently hard for a feller to cut (9)
27 Secret-service man who needs to be smart at absorbing information (5)
28 The disheartened and dishevelled masters who drive trucks along U.S. highways (9)
29 A loafer who works while others sleep? (5)

Down

1 Bomb-proof chambers for brief-sharing barristers? (9)
2 The stamina that took Shackleton on one of his expeditions (9)
3 Call round (4)
4 A roadside filling station? (9, 4)
5 Engineers circling at speed (4)
6 Upper-class liner, or its war-time enemy? (1-4)
7 Small place that hopes to draw record crowds (5)
10 Two dice throws soon over? (5, 2, 6)
14 Gets a review put on show (5)
15 He reverses an interdict about an Irish playwright (5)
17 A tyke we'd love to distraction seven days from now (5, 4)
18 He functions as a director of course (9)
20 A garment not easy to get out of? (5)

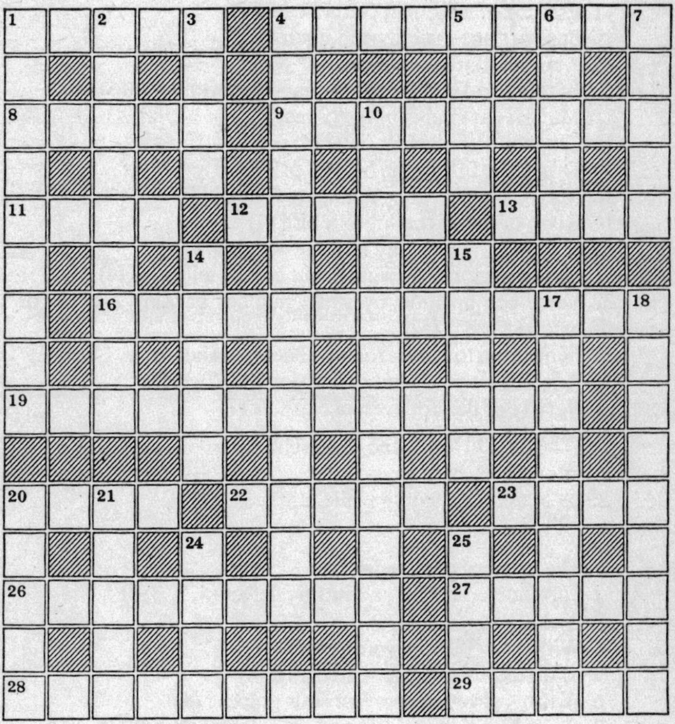

21 Ring an agent up if you want a seat for it at Covent Garden (5)
24 The fluency for which Oxford is renowned (4)
25 Master of the 12 was this innocent young skipper (4)

78

Across

1 Essence of a Roman Catholic text (7)
5 Support one may depend upon (5-2)
9 Another Garden of Eden? (7, 8)
10 Initially an English island connected with a State (4)
11 Material as coal is in retrospect (5)
12 Cheerful FBI agent's boy? (4)
15 Dispatched from the field of play (4, 3)
16 Maybe blemished by changing instead (7)
17 River of little account to a bird (7)
19 It sounds like destiny on four wheels (7)
21 Shows personal disregard that can be injurious (4)
22 Verse composition by small number backing a place of entertainment (5)
23 Something to chew around a Pacific island (4)
26 Affected by profound depression? (4, 2, 3, 6)
27 Variety of flax for everyone to sow (7)
28 Makes a comeback profitable? (7)

Down

1 The reverses of friends (7)
2 Surrendered rubber, admitting defeat (5, 2, 3, 5)
3 A shot grey (4)
4 Without a 3 felt as you were (7)
5 Main dishes of oyster-catchers (3-4)
6 Was his covetousness just sour grapes? (4)
7 One who exercises authority at a dental school? (5, 10)
8 In a word, synonymous with 2 (7)
13 A flower of France, and . . . (5)
14 . . . a West-country one, in part a marigold (5)
17 Song about a cad in old Greece (7)
18 Acknowledge a leading pressman briefly and get knotted! (7)
19 One ripe to set out to explore (7)
20 She could suitably punish 1 down with a change of point (7)
24 Union member (4)
25 Fitting for an assembly (4)

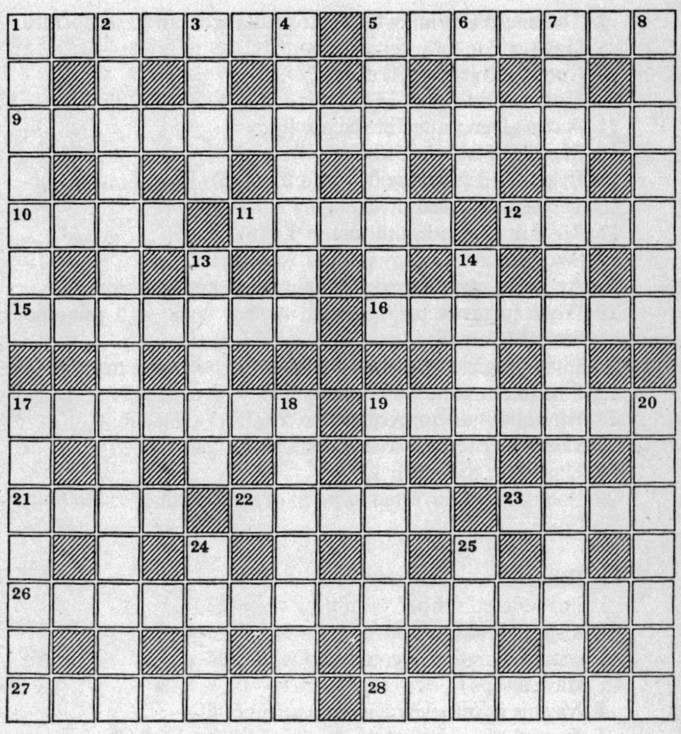

79

Across

1 The margin within which astronauts are trained to operate (5, 5)
9 Constructive idea (4)
10 Unfair conditions (3, 7)
11 A clip given a twirl at the top (6)
12 Make a note of deposit (3, 4)
15 Evidently hasn't a good word to say for beers brewed outside Great Britain! (7)
16 We'd first see what the cattle did (5)
17 See 3 down
18 An outer cover supplied within the motor industry (4)
19 'Then turn not pale, beloved — but come and join the dance' (Carroll: *Alice in Wonderland*) (5)
21 Elves or fairies that have a heavy duty laid upon them (7)
22 Sort of feminine habit that is highly revealing (7)
24 Row about doctor required to construct a log-cabin (6)
27 The fielder to deal with the matter at issue? (5, 5)
28 Unable to move quickly (4)
29 Poet slowly converted to point of most distinct vision (6-4)

Down

2 Top-drawer footnote about a fabulous poisoner (4)
3 and 17 across Limerick man who drew extensively on his travels (6, 4)
4 Marine fauna of Wales reclassified (3-4)
5 Painful consequence of a spell of hard labour? (4)
6 Irate tip about changing gear (7)
7 Not what the censor uses when he decides to cut a film (5-5)
8 An idle loss dispersed in every direction (2, 3, 5)
12 Successfully tackles a removal job? (5, 2, 3)
13 Divine lady to whom Sophocles turned for inspiration (6, 4)
14 Vengeful female trio who came from Scandinavia and not Nova Scotia (5)
15 In tranquillity I have another shot at the exam (5)
19 Rather too formal a description of a potato diet (7)
20 Bluejackets accommodated in a cool resort in Switzerland (7)

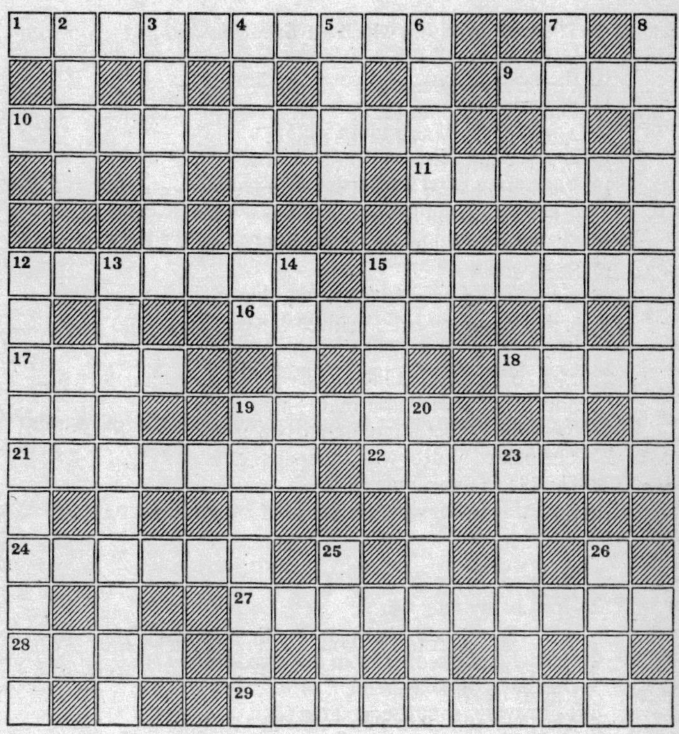

23 In sunny lands they grow oddly solemn (6)
25 Surrey men are at home there (4)
26 Ruin the United Nations likewise supported (4)

80

Across

1 They are anything but floating capital (7-5)
9 Given a tip not put on one side (2-5)
10 Its reel is designed for catching salmon (7)
11 Prima donna making an eager comeback (4)
12 The address of two mothers (5)
13 Knave who gives a lift to motorists (4)
16 Vegetables from the garden divested (7)
17 Sound old giant advises how to get rid of slackness (7)
18 He has the whip hand, having gone into the fight (7)
21 Secret serviceman? (7)
23 It takes little printed space (4)
24 Capacity that is five-sevenths of a quarter (5)
25 French I hesitate to mock (4)
28 Got close to replacing the dud held (7)
29 Tell ran back with speed (7)
30 Breaking a cane after being angry suggests lack of restraint (12)

Down

1 Put aside like a dresser (7)
2 Knot badly done (4)
3 Easterners usually associated with Westerns (7)
4 One who pressed a suit to vex a six-footer (7)
5 One basis of measurement (4)
6 Take away from French area (7)
7 Cw8 or 8st (13)
8 After being penniless then read anew how those who are may feel (6-7)
14 Anything that happens in the seventies (5)
15 A profit for the second time? (5)
19 Undergo treatment for reward (7)
20 Gather the bell has gone (5, 2)
21 He may lead his business associate a dance (7)
22 Mean to declare how old one is (7)
26 Feel moved to escape (4)
27 Nothing smuggled maybe, in Algeria (4)

80

1 2 3 4 5 6
7 8
9 10
11 12 13
14 15
16 17
18 19 20 21 22
23 24 25
26 27
28 29
30

The Solutions

No. 1

ACROSS – 1, Boycotter; 8, Smelling-salts; 11, Ashy; 12, Whoop; 13, Will; 16, Cutlass; 17, Tannery; 18, Chemist; 20, Monarch; 21, Late; 22, Prude; 23, Barn; 26, Decimal system; 27, Beanfeast.

DOWN – 2, Owls; 3, Clichés; 4, Tugboat; 5, Exam; 6, Amphitheatres; 7, Strike-breaker; 9, Catch cold; 10, Plaything; 14, Basin; 15, Anent; 19, Terrain; 20, Medusae; 24, Fine; 25, Asps.

No. 2

ACROSS – 1, As far as it goes; 10, Unnamed; 11, Greaser; 12, Loaf; 13, Sneak; 14, Ends; 17, Cremate; 18, Eastern; 19, Overdue; 22, Neither; 24, Imps; 25, Crewe; 26, Graf; 29, Acreage; 30, Arizona; 31, Loses the scent.

DOWN – 2, Santa Fé; 3, Aims; 4, Andante; 5, Ingrate; 6, Goes; 7, Essence; 8, Public holiday; 9, Prisoner of war; 15, Garda; 16, Aspic; 20, Esparto; 21, Earnest; 22, Newgate; 23, Harpoon; 27, Wake; 28, Disc.

No. 3

ACROSS – 1, Bearskin; 5, Adages; 9, Penelope; 10, Banner; 11, Draughts; 12, Solemn; 14, Second-hand; 18, Barleycorn; 22, Novice; 23, Left-hand; 24, Zodiac; 25, Amenable; 26, Rarity; 27, Interest.

DOWN – 1, Bipeds; 2, Anneal; 3, Silage; 4, Impatience; 6, Diamonds; 7, Gun-metal; 8, Serenade; 13, Journeyman; 15, Ebenezer; 16, Provider; 17, Penchant; 19, At once; 20, Rabble; 21, Advert.

No. 4

ACROSS – 1 and 9, Made a song about it; 10, Snorter; 11, Origami; 12, Gladiator; 14, Remedial; 15, Tromsö; 17, Another; 20, Aspens; 23, Producer; 25, Lying down; 26, Estonia; 27, Ant-lion; 28, Arrange; 29, Dissident.

DOWN – 2, Annular; 3, Earldom; 4, Sheraton; 5, Galore; 6, Domineers; 7, Stearin; 8, Stainless; 13, Oratory; 15, Temple Bar; 16, Saturnine; 18, Earnings; 19, Posters; 21, Paddled; 22, New moon; 24, Elated.

No. 5

ACROSS – 7, Notwithstanding; 8, Pillage; 10, Reviled; 11, Eager; 12, Devon; 14, Harps; 15, West; 16, Toil; 17, Rush; 19, Hide; 21, Ashes; 22, Snout; 23, Haunt; 25, Bail out; 26, Trieste; 27, Electrification.

DOWN – 1, Police-constable; 2, Swallow; 3, Stage; 4, Baker; 5, Admiral; 6, Under-production; 9, East; 10, Rest; 13, Negus; 14, Hinds; 17, Reflect; 18, Heat; 19, Hunt; 20, Entente; 23, Hurry; 24, Track.

No. 6

ACROSS – 1, Programme; 9, Come out; 10, Spotter; 11, Raeburn; 12, Mine-shaft; 14, Resigned; 15, Lasses; 17, Attempt; 20, Legend; 23, Spray-gun; 25, Pedometer; 26, Neither; 27, Details; 28, America; 29, Rare beast.

DOWN – 2, Replica; 3, Gutters; 4, Amethyst; 5, Ecarté; 6, Immediate; 7, Columns; 8, Stone-dead; 13, Free one; 15, Low Sunday; 16, Easy-chair; 18, Pliocene; 19, Praised; 21, Grenade; 22, Needles; 24, Uproar.

No. 7

ACROSS – 1, Library books; 8, Ontario; 9, Enteric; 11, Iceberg; 12, Drifter; 13, Yo-yos; 14, Impudence; 16, Odd moment; 19, Aesop; 21, Damaged; 23, Hessian; 24, Roseate; 25, Relieve; 26, Wedding-dress.

DOWN – 1, Lithely; 2, Bargees; 3, Alongside; 4, Yield; 5, Outvied; 6, Keratin; 7, Policy-holder; 10, Corresponded; 15, Pot the red; 17, Demesne; 18, On guard; 19, Absolve; 20, Shivers; 22, Due in.

No. 8

ACROSS – 1, Shadow-boxer; 9, Parr; 10, Nosey Parker; 11, Echo; 14, Orating; 16, Tosspot; 17, Gamin; 18, Nova; 19, Brie; 20, Sleep; 22, Naughty; 23, Silesia; 24, Gath; 28, Annie Oakley; 29, Punt; 30, Wealthiness.

DOWN – 2, Hoof; 3, Does; 4, Wapping; 5, Ours; 6, Erewhon; 7, Catch-phrase; 8, Arm of the law; 12, Corn in Egypt; 13, Fan vaulting; 15, Gaily; 16, Times; 20, Strange; 21, Pibroch; 25, Dial; 26, Skin; 27, Mews.

No. 9

ACROSS – 1, Headlights; 8, Unawed; 9, On the links; 10, Andrew; 11, Workington; 12, Ninety; 13, Aria; 15, Mastiff; 19, Chicory; 21, Atte; 22, Jovial; 25, Dollar bill; 27, Athene; 28, Rear window; 29, Portia; 30, Light tread.

DOWN – 1, Hook-worm; 2, Actors; 3, Liebig; 4, Going; 5, Susannah; 6, Sardonic; 7, Deventer; 13, Aft; 14, Ice; 16, Adoption; 17, Tridents; 18, Falderal; 20, Yellowed; 23, Artist; 24, Fiddle; 26, Lurch.

No. 10

ACROSS – 1, Standing army; 8, Pass out; 9, Polacks; 12, Rhea; 13, Lover; 14, Pump; 17, In short; 18, Smother; 19, Going up; 22, Scratch; 24, Leek; 25, Madam; 26, Liar; 29, Gallant; 31, Imagine; 32, Double vision.

DOWN – 1, Sisters; 2, Atom; 3, Detroit; 4, Napless; 5, Able; 6, Yak; 7, Sparking-plug; 10, Cough; 11, Supercharger; 15, Tough; 16, Board; 20, Ideal; 21, Piastre; 22, Swahili; 23, Tuition; 27, Lamb; 28, Bali; 30, Add.

No. 11

ACROSS – 1, Half-nelson; 6, Awls; 10, Liver; 11, South Pole; 12, Imbecile; 13, Light; 15, Letting; 17, Torture; 19, Mahatma; 21, Centaur; 22, Niger; 24, El Dorado; 27, Telescope; 28, Gnome; 29, Dope; 30, News-stands.

DOWN – 1, Halt; 2, Love-match; 3, Nerve; 4, Lasting; 5, Opulent; 7, Wrong; 8, Sweetheart; 9, Children; 14, Eliminated; 16, Interest; 18, Up and down; 20, Anemone; 21, Cadgers; 23, Galop; 25, Right; 26, Keys.

No. 12

ACROSS – 1 and 5, Lantern lecture; 9, Vast improvement; 10, Obol; 11, Solid; 12, Duel; 15, Keep out; 16, Gorilla; 17, Punkahs; 19, Tractor; 21, Tout; 22, Hippy; 23, Bung; 26, Hand-to-hand fight; 27, Tidings; 28, Tessera.

DOWN – 1, Live-oak; 2, No stone unturned; 3, Elia; 4, Nips out; 5, Looting; 6, Clef; 7, Unequal struggle; 8, Estella; 13, Foray; 14, Great; 17, Pot-shot; 18, Swishes; 19, Top-knot; 20, Regatta; 24, Stun; 25, Efts.

No. 13

ACROSS – 1 and 5, Contract bridge; 9, Billy-can; 10, Scored; 12, Redressed; 13, Reign; 14, Eric; 16, Shingle; 19, Abetter; 21, Olga; 24, Anode; 25, Campanile; 27, Innate; 28, Brighton; 29, Reside; 30, Philomel.

DOWN – 1, Coburg; 2, No lady; 3, Rhyme; 4 and 20, Classic race; 6 and 26, Recording angel; 7, Darlings; 8, Endanger; 11 and 21 down, Ides of March; 15, Retreated; 17, Cavalier; 18, Recounts; 20, See 4; 21, See 11; 22, Victim; 23, Kennel; 26, See 6.

No. 14

ACROSS – 1, Not right; 5, Sly dog; 9, Bastille; 10, Impair; 11, Laureate; 12, Inform; 14, Brain drain; 18, Reapproach; 22, Bolero; 23, Agrarian; 24, Noodle; 25, Governor; 26, Steady; 27, Very nice.

DOWN – 1, No-ball; 2, Tissue; 3, Irises; 4, Holy terror; 6, Lemonade; 7, Dragoman; 8, Garamond; 13, Birch grove; 15, Tribunes; 16, Calliope; 17, Sparkled; 19, Napery; 20, Rienzi; 21, Unfree.

No. 15

ACROSS – 1, Movable feast; 8, Hundred; 9, Gas-lamp; 11, Rolling; 12, Trapper; 13, Chant; 14, Angle-iron; 16, Remainder; 19, Local; 21, Unnoted; 23, Sagging; 24, Thinner; 25, Omnibus; 26, Interspersed.

DOWN – 1, Manilla; 2, Verdict; 3, Bodyguard; 4, Eight; 5, Enslave; 6, Scamper; 7, Short-circuit; 10, Phrenologist; 15, Gyroscope; 17, Mansion; 18, Intense; 19, Legends; 20, Cribbed; 22, Darts.

No. 16

ACROSS – 1, Shortcoming; 8, Proposition; 11, Male; 12, Nero; 13, Abstain; 15, New Year; 16, Topes; 17, Shed; 18, Asia; 19, Defer; 21, Doctors; 22, Relayed; 23, Rasp; 26, Time; 27, Tape-measure; 28, Press-button.

DOWN – 2, Hire; 3, Reposit; 4, Cost; 5, Mottoes; 6, Noon; 7, Ambassadors; 8, Plaster cast; 9, Never say die; 10, Door-handles; 14, Notes; 15, Never; 19, Drovers; 20, Revisit; 24, Pair; 25, Herb; 26, Trio.

No. 17

ACROSS – 1, Hindsight; 8, Smothered mate; 11, Rains; 12, Radii; 13, Opine; 16, Cretan; 17, Beat it; 18, Erato; 19, Rating; 20, Nemean; 21, Allay; 24, North; 26, Rates; 27, Static warfare; 28, Headlines.

DOWN – 2, Iotas; 3, Drew up; 4, Iceman; 5, Hamar; 6, Ambidexterity; 7, Study the stars; 9, Procuring; 10, Kittenish; 13, Onega; 14, In all; 15, Ebony; 22, Lanced; 23, Alkali; 25, Hythe; 26, Rifle.

No. 18

ACROSS – 1, Reseda; 4, Swanking; 9, Filled; 10, Disciple; 12, Ruth; 13, Blasé; 14, Scut; 17, Front benches; 20, Social unrest; 23, Boon; 24, Agate; 25, Carp; 28, Outstrip; 29, Seaton; 30, Bone idle; 31, Howdah.

DOWN – 1, Riff-raff; 2, Solution; 3, Deer; 5, Whimsicality; 6, Nick; 7, Impact; 8, Ghetto; 11, Sleeping-pill; 15, Strop; 16, Peony; 18, Departed; 19, At a pinch; 21, Absorb; 22, Bolton; 26, Etui; 27, Hero.

No. 19

ACROSS – 1, Pilot schemes; 8, Narrate; 9, Sleeper; 11, Unswept; 12, Sinking; 13, Masks; 14, Enceladus; 16, Nominates; 19, Briar; 21, Hair-net; 23, Against; 24, Patient; 25, Embargo; 26, Spanish Steps.

DOWN – 1, Purists; 2, Leaders; 3, Treatment; 4, Casks; 5, Eternal; 6, Emptied; 7, One-upmanship; 10, Registration; 15, Castanets; 17, Maintop; 18, Nankeen; 19, Bramble; 20, Ignores; 22, Titus.

No. 20

ACROSS – 1, Punch-ball; 9, Menace; 10, Good hands; 11, Adonis; 12, Live-wires; 13, Scrape; 17, Act; 19, Bid one good-night; 20, Amp; 21, Ninety; 25, Fairy tale; 26, Ormolu; 27, Mischiefs; 28, Eyelet; 29, Interests.

DOWN – 2, Utopia; 3, Cadres; 4, Brazil; 5, Ladies' companion; 6, Mendicant; 7, Rain-gauge; 8, Bed-sheets; 14, Abandoned; 15, Odd number; 16, Installed; 17, Aga; 18, Top; 22, Crèche; 23, Strike; 24, Ill fit.

No. 21

ACROSS – 1, Type; 3, Adage; 6, Step; 11, Auction; 12, Retract; 13, Flight of fancy; 16, Redwood; 17, Eagerly; 18, Doormat; 21, Pitfall; 23, Standing order; 26, Project; 27, Animate; 28, Rake; 29, Cells; 30, Deal.

DOWN – 1, Trap; 2, Pickled; 4, Denoted; 5, Giraffe; 7, Tram-car; 8, Pitt; 9, Wing-commander; 10, Straight grain; 14, Bride; 15, Myall; 19, Outlook; 20, Thistle; 21, Pigtail; 22, Average; 24, Spar; 25, Teal.

No. 22

ACROSS – 1, Amusement; 9, Emirate; 10, Cynthia; 11, Unnerve; 12, Pompadour; 14, New heart; 15, Beanos; 17, Cheetah; 20, Cabral; 23, Overload; 25, Pyromania; 26, Counsel; 27, Stylite; 28, Sea-room; 29, Bob-cherry.

DOWN – 2, Maypole; 3, Set upon; 4, Main dish; 5, Tenure; 6, Minnehaha; 7, Fairway; 8, Resentful; 13, Unready; 15, Below cost; 16, Occlusion; 18, Acrostic; 19, Setubal; 21, Braille; 22, Aviator; 24, Aplomb.

No. 23

ACROSS – 1, Right-hand man; 8, Andante; 9, Commons; 12, Able; 13, Befit; 14, Glee; 17, Redraft; 18, Example; 19, Scruple; 22, Morocco; 24, Ruby; 25, Crash; 26, Alec; 29, Elspeth; 31, Nurture; 32, Evening class.

DOWN – 1, Riddled; 2, Gang; 3, Thereat; 4, Ascribe; 5, Dump; 6, Nun; 7, Naval reserve; 10, Orlop; 11, Skeleton crew; 15, Wasps; 16, Harry; 20, Rebus; 21, Earthen; 22, Masonic; 23, Colours; 27, Keen; 28, Area; 30, Lee.

No. 24

ACROSS – 5, Joists; 8, Canon law; 9, Rubicon; 10, Freda; 11, Caithness; 13, Smoother; 14, Lupine; 17, Lap; 19, Gyp; 20, Delays; 23, Choosers; 26, Aggregate; 28, Niger; 29, Swallow; 30, Chartres; 31, Ashore.

DOWN – 1, Scoffs; 2, Antenor; 3, Unearthly; 4, Palace; 5, Jauntily; 6, Ixion; 7, Thousand; 12, Arc; 15, Up-country; 16, Tea-gowns; 18, Ash Grove; 21, Act; 22, Beggars; 24, Height; 25, Stress; 27, Rollo.

No. 25

ACROSS – 1, Chain reaction; 10, Russian; 11, Comrade; 12, Maid; 13, Sweep; 14, Fist; 17, Adenoid; 18, Trainer; 19, Set sail; 22, Frame-up; 24, Hour; 25, March; 26, Bent; 29, On trial; 30, Station; 31, Secret passage.

DOWN – 2, Hostile; 3, Ibid; 4, Renewed; 5, Ancient; 6, Tome; 7, Oration; 8, Grammar school; 9, Letters-patent; 15, Woman; 16, Banal; 20, Trustee; 21, Leaflet; 22, Fuchsia; 23, Evening; 27, Liar; 28, Mars.

No. 26

ACROSS – 1, Throttle; 5, Spared; 9, Radiator; 10, Radium; 11, Diameter; 12, Stolen; 14, Court-cards; 18, Blackheads; 22, Tramps; 23, Fleabite; 24, Unseat; 25, Lean year; 26, Eureka; 27, Florists.

DOWN – 1, Tirade; 2, Red man; 3, Thanet; 4, Looked over; 6, Practice; 7, Raillery; 8, Demonism; 13, Bridal veil; 15, Abstruse; 16, Macassar; 17, Skipjack; 19, Manner; 20, Divers; 21, Hearts.

No. 27

ACROSS – 1, Genealogist; 9, Ludo; 10, Wensleydale; 11, This; 14, Heating; 16, Brushed; 17, Gabon; 18, Tied; 19, Scar; 20, Spahi; 22, Ignores; 23, Ancient; 24, Gust; 28, Fingerprint; 29, Open; 30, Desecration.

DOWN – 2, Ever; 3, Easy; 4, Leering; 5, Gods; 6, Silvern; 7, Bushwhacker; 8, Considerate; 12, Whittington; 13, Paternoster; 15, Gasps; 16, Botha; 20, Service; 21, Insurer; 25, Ague; 26, Fret; 27, Undo.

No. 28

ACROSS – 1, Treadmill; 8, Walking-on part; 11, Rear; 12, Bruin; 13, Mali; 16, Measure; 17, Guerdon; 18, Apparel; 20, Milksop; 21, Oval; 22, Maine; 23, Tree; 26, Beginner's luck; 27, Sword-play.

DOWN – 2, Rake; 3, Aintree; 4, Mooning; 5, Lope; 6, Faraway places; 7, Urban district; 9, Drum-major; 10, Kidnapped; 14, Query; 15, Wells; 19, Learner; 20, Mantrap; 24, View; 25, Elia.

No. 29

ACROSS – 8, Pure; 9, Nut; 10, Arthur; 11, Moloch; 12, Noisette; 13, Canterbury Tales; 15, Defarge; 17, Bargain; 20, Caught red-handed; 23, Knitting; 25, Railed; 26, Canute; 27, Ron; 28, Evil.

DOWN – 1, Cupola; 2, Lemon tea; 3, On the right lines; 4, Stand up; 5, Family gathering; 6, Stresa; 7, Punt; 14, Eli; 16, Era; 18, Gentiles; 19, Beggary; 21, Get out; 22, Eyelid; 24, Neat.

No. 30

ACROSS – 8, Intone; 9, Airtight; 10, Absorb; 11, Exacting; 12, Eon; 13, Tosser; 14, Theories; 16, Realism; 18, Rubbers; 23, Bordered; 27, Pagoda; 28, Are; 29, Chromium; 30, Rumble; 31, Prussian; 32, Unsung.

DOWN – 1, One by one; 2, Colossal; 3, Cerberus; 4, Talents; 5, Urbane; 6, Titter; 7, Change; 15, Orb; 17, Ire; 19, Upper-cut; 20, Bigamist; 21, Redolent; 22, Adamant; 24, Others; 25, Drowsy; 26, Raisin.

No. 31

ACROSS – 1, Revocation; 6, Arum; 10, Forge; 11, Muffin-man; 12, Flat-iron; 13, Donor; 15, Magical; 17, Elastic; 19, Letters; 21, Ethical; 22, Homer; 24, Athletic; 27, Unfounded; 28, Reign; 29, Slim; 30, Clean hands.

DOWN – 1, Raft; 2, Very light; 3, Chest; 4, Tumbrel; 5, Offence; 7, Roman; 8, Minor scale; 9 Bird-bath; 14, Small hours; 16, Clear out; 18, Tactician; 20, Scandal; 21, Echidna; 23, Mufti; 25, Earth; 26, Onus.

No. 32

ACROSS – 5, Jemima; 8, Cottager; 9, Actress; 10, Roves; 11, Cambodian; 13, Herb-beer; 14, Apples; 17, Lex; 19, Ana; 20, Occult; 23, Passport; 26, Outhouses; 28, Orbit; 29, Wallace; 30, Mind's eye; 31, In vain.

DOWN – 1, Scorch; 2, Stivers; 3, Daisy Bell; 4, Menace; 5, Jacobean; 6, Mired; 7, Mistakes; 12, Arm; 15, Passwords; 16, Schumann; 18, Etruscan; 21, Ape; 22, Cobbler; 24, Assoil; 25, Totter; 27, Halma.

No. 33

ACROSS – 1, Best man; 5, Refrain; 9, Swallow; 10, Emanate; 11, Alms-house; 12, Sinai; 13, Dodge; 15, No quarter; 17 and 19, As good as a feast; 22, Ideal; 23, Bird's-nest; 25, Bunkers; 26, Mention; 27, Erratic; 28, Nirvana.

DOWN – 1, Bustard; 2, Swarmed; 3, Mulch; 4, New Guinea; 5, Reeve; 6, Flagstaff; 7, Against; 8, Needier; 14, Emollient; 16, Quarryman; 17, Amiable; 18, Gleaner; 20, America; 21, Titania; 23, Basic; 24, Señor.

No. 34

ACROSS – 1, Megalomaniac; 8, Utrillo; 9, Methane; 11, Trident; 12, Epicarp; 13, Onion; 14, Meat-eater; 16, Real world; 19, Truro; 21, Ensigns; 23, Lurcher; 24, Foggier; 25, Slogans; 26, Light-hearted.

DOWN – 1, Martini; 2, Galleon; 3, Lion-tamer; 4, Mamie; 5, Nitrite; 6, Adamant; 7, Suit yourself; 10, Esparto grass; 15, Andalusia; 17, Assegai; 18, Waggish; 19, Turn out; 20, Unheard; 22, Sarah.

No. 35

ACROSS – 1, Vanity-case; 6, Disc; 9, Tennis-ball; 10, Peru; 13, Slender; 15, Income; 16, Relict; 17, Join the majority; 18, Icemen; 20, Faille; 21, Nominal; 22, Tote; 25, Mastership; 26, Dill; 27, Terrorists.

DOWN – 1, Vats; 2, Nuns; 3, Trifle; 4, Cabinet minister; 5, Salver; 7, Ineligible; 8, Countrymen; 11, Disjointed; 12, Accidental; 13, Smitten; 14, Removal; 19, Nonage; 20, Fairer; 23, Thus; 24, Opus.

No. 36

ACROSS – 1, Part-time; 5, Pasted; 9, Tapeworm; 10, Adagio; 11, Emigrant; 13, Feet up; 14, Ear; 16, Access; 19, Disease; 20, Magnet; 21, Tub; 26, Oliver; 27, Turncoat; 28, Thirty; 29, Striking; 30, Liners; 31, Freehold.

DOWN – 1, Patter; 2, Repair; 3, Towers; 4, Marine; 6, Audience; 7, Together; 8, Doorpost; 12, Take out; 15, Fit; 16, Ass; 17, Immortal; 18, Ignition; 19, Deserter; 22, Butter; 23, Endive; 24, Domino; 25, Staged.

No. 37

ACROSS – 1, Ash blonde; 9, Memento; 10, Abraded; 11, Otranto; 12, Disturbed; 14, Symbolic; 15, Asleep; 17, Leveret; 20, Mysore; 23, Card-vote; 25, Isinglass; 26, Nepotic; 27, Annelid; 28, Acetone; 29, Take my tip.

DOWN – 2, Submits; 3, Brattle; 4, Overripe; 5, Embody; 6, Improbity; 7, Inanely; 8, Motorcade; 13, Essenes; 15, Anacondas; 16, Elevation; 18, Eminence; 19, Prophet; 21, Sillery; 22, Rossini; 24, Ticket.

No. 38

ACROSS – 6, Sportsmanship; 8, Pistol; 9, Edentate; 10, Wit; 11, Strata; 12, Undercut; 14, Mandate; 16, Stylite; 20, Free beer; 23, Ravage; 24, Lot; 25, In a trice; 26, Aerial; 27, Elephantiasis.

DOWN – 1, Port Said; 2, Stalwart; 3, Impetus; 4, Indeed; 5, Whiter; 6, Saint Lawrence; 7, Put out to grass; 13, Ely; 15, Alb; 17, Tartaric; 18, Liverish; 19, Orleans; 21, Entrée; 22, Elisha.

No. 39

ACROSS – 1, Mutton-heads; 8, Go through it; 11, Oxon; 12, Tale; 13, Medical; 15, Demerit; 16, Noyes; 17, Part; 18, Bait; 19, Ad-lib; 21, Gathers; 22, Teacher; 23, Onus; 26, Alan; 27, Point of time; 28, Bell-wethers.

DOWN – 2, Upon; 3, Teheran; 4, Noon; 5, Engines; 6, Doit; 7, Not my pigeon; 8, Good write-up; 9, Tarry awhile; 10, Petty tyrant; 14, Lord's; 15, Debit; 19, Arsenal; 20, Bewitch; 24, Sole; 25, Sore; 26, Amir.

No. 40

ACROSS – 1, Attestation; 9, Zero; 10, Unqualified; 11, Spin; 14, Darling; 16, Reverse; 17, Galop; 18, Abut; 19, Stop; 20, Seals; 22, Cohorts; 23, Sporran; 24, Miss; 28, Straightway; 29, Neat; 30, Orchestrate.

DOWN – 2, Tent; 3, Emus; 4, Telling; 5, Taft; 6, Onestep; 7, Temperature; 8, Counterpane; 12, Advancement; 13, Draughtsman; 15, Gales; 16, Rolls; 20, Starter; 21, Sponges; 25, Path; 26, Stir; 27, Fast.

No. 41

ACROSS – 1, Steamed; 5, March up; 9, Madcaps; 10, Growler; 11, Level best; 12, Robes; 13, Roses; 15, Laminated; 17, High tides; 19, Earth; 22, Twill; 23, Pretender; 25, Hostile; 26, Gallows; 27, Dryness; 28, Rosella.

DOWN – 1, Sampler; 2, Endives; 3, Myall; 4, Dispelled; 5, Might; 6, Rio Grande; 7, Halibut; 8, Perused; 14, Satellite; 16, Messenger; 17, Hatched; 18, Gainsay; 20, Redpoll; 21, Hornsea; 23, Press; 24, Ellis.

No. 42

ACROSS – 1, Constable; 8, Cobbled street; 11, Hedge; 12, Drone; 13, Trams; 16, Rarity; 17, Candid; 18, Roger; 19, Onside; 20, Adhere; 21, Steep; 24, Aheap; 26, Copse; 27, Strong current; 28, Pyrethrum.

DOWN – 2, Ombre; 3, Skewer; 4, Anselm; 5, Lurid; 6, Good prospects; 7, Second helping; 9, Charwoman; 10, Beady-eyed; 13, Tyres; 14, Angle; 15, Scrap; 22, Tangle; 23, Enough; 25, Peony; 26, Corfu.

No. 43

ACROSS – 1, Grouse season; 9, Release; 10, Leander; 11, Ivan; 12, Lists; 13, Firm; 16, Tatters; 17, Serpent; 18, Railing; 21, Scuttle; 23, Fast; 24, Edgar; 25, Slav; 28, Erasure; 29, Laconic; 30, Closing words.

DOWN – 1, Gallant; 2, Oval; 3. Species; 4, Salutes; 5, Adam; 6, Old-time; 7, Artists' Rifles; 8, Prompt service; 14, Lewis; 15, Argus; 19, Install; 20, Gudgeon; 21, Shallow; 22, Talents; 26, Cuts; 27, Scar.

No. 44

ACROSS – 1, Oligarch; 5, Shires; 9, Decadent; 10, Presto; 11, Almoners; 12, Annual; 14, Act of Union; 18, Ilfracombe; 22, Lottie; 23, El Dorado; 24, Masque; 25, Minister; 26. Shandy; 27, Agonised.

DOWN – 1, Oldham; 2, Income; 3, Ardent; 4, Contractor; 6, Harangue; 7, Rasputin; 8. Scotland; 13, Top billing; 15, Gig-lamps; 16, Off to sea; 17, Fatigued; 19, Lotion; 20, Mantis; 21, Soared.

No. 45

ACROSS – 1, Lessors; 5, Flotsam; 9, To the manner born; 10, Raid; 11, Begot; 12, Star; 15, Legally; 16, Tenants; 17, Concert; 19, Plum jam; 21, Avon; 22, Snick; 23, Aced; 26, Private soldiers; 27, Ring out; 28, Oversee.

DOWN – 1, Lateral; 2, Setting in motion; 3, Over; 4, Stately; 5, Find out; 6, Oars; 7, Shooting-jackets; 8, Manures; 13, Sleep; 14, Snout; 17, Clapper; 18, Tangent; 19, Piccolo; 20, Modiste; 24, Sago; 25, Adze.

No. 46

ACROSS – 1, Keeping watch; 8, Omnibus; 9, Ascents; 11, Siddons; 12, Despise; 13, Woman; 14, Esperanto; 16, Realistic; 19, Biter; 21, Insists; 23, Drawn up; 24, Garbage; 25, Imagine; 26, Fast and loose.

DOWN – 1, Kingdom; 2, Embrown; 3, Insistent; 4, Grand; 5, Accuser; 6, Consign; 7, House-warming; 10, Stenographer; 15, Pack-drill; 17, Austria; 18, Instant; 19, Bravado; 20, Tensile; 22, Stern.

No. 47

ACROSS – 1, Calibrate; 9, Indaba; 10, Barricade; 11, Mongol; 12, Tarpaulin; 13, Repair; 17, Aga; 19, Red hand; 20, Chaplin; 21, Ate; 23, Abroad; 27, Amaryllis; 28, Bemoan; 29, Many-sided; 30, Rental; 31, Minnesota.

DOWN – 2, Abadan; 3, Irrupt; 4, Recoup; 5, Tidying; 6, Income tax; 7, Laughable; 8, Tailoring; 14, Friar-bird; 15, Adornment; 16, Catamaran; 17, Ada; 18, Ace; 22, Timpani; 24, Crayon; 25, Plains; 26, Digest.

No. 48

ACROSS – 7, Automatic; 8, Ergot; 10, Great Tom; 11, Oberon; 12, Pâté; 13, Not so bad; 15 and 17, Arguing the toss; 20, Half-hose; 22, Dirk; 25, Oboist; 26, Dabbling; 27, Rally; 28, In passing.

DOWN – 1, Curry; 2, Sonata; 3, Pantheon; 4 and 19, Diamond wedding; 5, Freeport; 6, Holocaust; 9, Port; 14, Broad-bean; 16, Unfairly; 18, Hudibras; 19, See 4; 21, Orts; 23, Relish; 24, Anona.

No. 49

ACROSS – 1, Rough-rider; 9, Liar; 10, On all sides; 11, Tomtit; 12, Lapping; 15, Tersely; 16, Go far; 17, 18 and 7 down, Mary had a little lamb; 19, Felon; 21, Orchard; 22, Toll-bar; 24, Calves; 27, Hornblower; 28, Arum; 29, Travestied.

DOWN – 2, Owns; 3, Gallop; 4, Resting; 5, Dido; 6, Rustler; 7, See 17 across; 8, Pretty fair; 12, Lump of clay; 13, Paracelsus; 14, Gored; 15, Tarot; 19, Freshet; 20, Notable; 23, Let out; 25, Aria; 26, Mere.

No. 50

ACROSS – 1, Silverside; 6, Slew; 9, Right angle; 10, Bait; 13, Invited; 15, Tyrant; 16, Tipper; 17, Crime of violence; 18, Reward; 20, Empire; 21, Savanna; 22, Dive; 25, Sphericity; 26, Rise; 27, Crossed out.

DOWN – 1, Sire; 2, Logs; 3, Extent; 4, Sensitive papers; 5, Dulcet; 7, Lead pencil; 8, Water-level; 11, Stock-rider; 12, Brainwaves; 13, In tears; 14, Diploma; 19, Damper; 20, Entire; 23, Lido; 24, Ryot.

No. 51

ACROSS – 1, Springboard; 8, House of Keys; 11, Loot; 12, Stye; 13, Cedilla; 15, Pyramid; 16, Lines; 17, Runs; 18, Clan; 19, Mecca; 21, Cobbled; 22, Erratic; 23, Arcs; 26, Sock; 27, Knocked down; 28, Spirit-lamps.

DOWN – 2, Plot; 3, Install; 4, Good; 5, Orkneys; 6, Rays; 7, Electrician; 8, Holding back; 9, Stimulation; 10, Wedding-cake; 14, Aired; 15, Peace; 19, Menacer; 20, Arcadia; 24, Snap; 25, Feet; 26, Swop.

No. 52

ACROSS – 8, Detached; 9, Amelia; 10, Obi; 11, Hamilcar; 12, Lieder; 13, Election address; 15, Parings; 18, Contest; 21, Loch Ness Monster; 24, Gibbet; 25, Huntress; 26, Hoe; 27, Settee; 28, Ancestry.

DOWN – 1, Retail; 2, Manioc; 3, Shocking weather; 4, Adoring; 5, Failed to connect; 6, Sewer-rat; 7, Diseases; 14, Err; 16, Atomiser; 17, Inhabits; 19, Eat; 20, Escheat; 22, Stresa; 23, Ensure.

No. 53

ACROSS – 1, Ever after; 8, Nursery garden; 11, Order; 12, There; 13, Other; 16, Wander; 17, Insult; 18, Aloof; 19, Nugget; 20, Lancer; 21, Elsie; 24, Ounce; 26, Titan; 27, Cut the painter; 28, Preserved.

DOWN – 2, Visor; 3, Rarest; 4, Figure; 5, Egret; 6, Budding genius; 7, Revenue-cutter; 9, Bow-window; 10, Nectarine; 13, Orate; 14, Hoops; 15, Rifle; 22, Likens; 23, Impair; 25, Enter; 26, Tense.

No. 54

ACROSS – 1, Insure; 4, Pastor; 10, Jupiter; 11, Overrun; 12, Eli; 13, Reels; 14, Twine; 15, Mermaid Tavern; 18, Feels the bumps; 23, Shied; 25, Vicar; 26, Era; 27, Cleaves; 28, Warlock; 29, Entity; 30, Letter.

DOWN – 1, Injury; 2, Supreme; 3, Rites; 5, Alert; 6, Terrier; 7, Runlet; 8, Great interest; 9, Doing the crawl; 16, Rye; 17, Elm; 19, Evident; 20, Pace out; 21, Psyche; 22, Broker; 24, Divot; 25, Verne.

No. 55

ACROSS – 5, Factor; 8, Chairman; 9, Oatmeal; 10, Ropes; 11, Retractor; 13, Dwelling; 14, Credit; 17, Rap; 19, Tea; 20, Crease; 23, Adjacent; 26, Local time; 28, Ideal; 29, Deleted; 30, Strutted; 31, Estate.

DOWN – 1, Scared; 2, Dappled; 3, Wrestlers; 4, Cavern; 5, Flat-race; 6, Comic; 7, Oratorio; 12, Ego; 15, Rapacious; 16, Triolets; 18, Aesthete; 21, Cam; 22, Deserts; 24, Dearth; 25, Toledo; 27, Arena.

No. 56

ACROSS – 1, Habitat; 5, Columns; 9, Phosphorescence; 10, Edda; 11, Sieve; 12, Disc; 15, Spy ring; 16, Dowager; 17, Taproom; 19, Coroner; 21, Edam; 22, Unlit; 23, Isn't; 26, Driving a bargain; 27, Engaged; 28, Repress.

DOWN – 1, Hapless; 2, Broadly speaking; 3, Tape; 4, Tooting; 5, Cleaved; 6, Lace; 7, Mending one's pace; 8, Spencer; 13, Bison; 14, Swarm; 17, Tweedle; 18, Managed; 19, Climber; 20, Ratings; 24, King; 25, Trip.

No. 57

ACROSS – 1, Flagstaff; 9, Mañana; 10, Foothills; 11, Tessie; 12, Minute-men; 13, Degree; 17, Ace; 19, Romantic Revival; 20, Tug; 21, Fiends; 25, Lake poets; 26, Sugary; 27, Bilingual; 28, Orissa; 29, Intestate.

DOWN – 2, Look in; 3, Get out; 4, Tailed; 5, False accusation; 6, Take leave; 7, Palsgrave; 8, Harebells; 14, Professor; 15, Ambergris; 16, Snodgrass; 17, Ait; 18, Erg; 22, Defile; 23, Sought; 24, At last.

No. 58

ACROSS – 7 and 8, Camel-hair brush; 10, Clematis; 11, Lascar; 12, Inns; 13, Immobile; 16, Espy; 18, Diagram; 20, Thawing; 22, Echo; 24, Idolater; 26, Rapt; 29, Vizier; 30, Zeppelin; 31, Helot; 32, New potato.

DOWN – 1, Dally; 2, Penman; 3, White Sea; 4, Airship; 5, Cross-bow; 6, Assailant; 9, Slam; 14, Myth; 15, Pied Piper; 17, Smee; 19, Gallipot; 21, Hornpipe; 23, Crozier; 25, Tyre; 27, Plenty; 28, Ditto.

No. 59

ACROSS – 1, Crack of dawn; 8, Crepuscular; 11, Okay; 12, Dull; 13, Deposit; 15, Rainbow; 16, Names; 17, Prim; 18, Brer; 19, Boxer; 21, Rangoon; 22, Let down; 23, Tars; 26, Peas; 27, Schoolgirls; 28, Switzerland.

DOWN – 2, Rory; 3 and 19, Captain Boycott; 4, Ossa; 5, Douglas; 6, Woad; 7, Good spirits; 8, Campaigners; 9, Rubber soles; 10, Floweriness; 14, Talon; 15, Rebel; 19, See 3; 20, Retrial; 24, Scow; 25, Glee; 26, Plan.

No. 60

ACROSS – 1, Stop-press; 8, Coming to terms; 11, Hands; 12, Theme; 13, Basra; 16, Primer; 17, Morsel; 18, Areca; 19, Tights; 20, Sponge; 21, Steps; 24, Clout; 26, Extra; 27, Assassination; 28, Apple-tart.

DOWN – 2, Trips; 3, Pagoda; 4, Roofer; 5, Sheet; 6, Counting-house; 7, Impersonation; 9, Chopstick; 10, Bell-metal; 13, Brass; 14, Swede; 15, Amass; 22, Tonsil; 23, Punnet; 25, Tramp; 26, Eater.

No. 61

ACROSS – 1, Overstatement; 10, Arsenic; 11, Addison; 12, In time; 15, Aspire; 16, Exhaust; 17, Earl; 18, Eggs; 19, Immoral; 20, Tack; 22, Alga; 24, Plunder; 26, Tumble; 27, Doomed; 30, Open-air; 31, Entrain; 32, Reception-room.

DOWN – 2, Visitor; 3, Rename; 4, Tick; 5, Trap; 6, Modest; 7, Nesting; 8, Manifestation; 9, Understanding; 13, Example; 14, Maroons; 15, Ashamed; 21, Compete; 23, Lumbago; 24, Please; 25, Roster; 28, Brat; 29, Zero.

No. 62

ACROSS – 1, On reflection; 8, Antonym; 9, Padstow; 11, Turmoil; 12, Look out; 13, Roost; 14, Carpenter; 16, Northerly; 19, Hydro; 21, Algeria; 23, Emptied; 24, Entreat; 25, Edifice; 26, Cat's-whiskers.

DOWN – 1, Ontario; 2, Ring out; 3, Family car; 4, Expel; 5, Tadpole; 6, Outpost; 7, Cast-iron case; 10, Water-soldier; 15, Rhymeless; 17, Regatta; 18, Hardens; 19, Hoplite; 20, Dailies; 22, Aitch.

No. 63

ACROSS – 1, Ghost town; 9, Ferret; 10, Annalists; 11, Avenue; 12, Blackburn; 13, Assent; 17, Aid; 19, Haunting refrain; 20, Thy; 21, Lupine; 25, Bagatelle; 26, Finery; 27, Cigarette; 28, Sienna; 29, Picketing.

DOWN – 2, Handle; 3, Scarce; 4, Trilby; 5, Watertight alibi; 6, Leaves off; 7, Orangeman; 8, Attesting; 14, Shellfish; 15, Suspended; 16, Itinerant; 17, Ant; 18, Dry; 22, Damask; 23, Desert; 24, Platan.

No. 64

ACROSS – 1, Swell idea; 8, First vision; 11, Alley; 12, Lotto; 13, Grits; 16, Ethane; 17, Witham; 18, Nesta; 19, Easter; 20, Manual; 21, Ennui; 24, Noise; 26, Hawks; 27, Cattle breeder; 28, Saddle-bag.

DOWN – 2, Wispy; 3, Ledger; 4 Invest; 5, Easel; 6, Field hospital; 7, Forty-hour week; 9, Madeleine; 10, Normalise; 13, Genre; 14, Ibsen; 15, Swami; 22, Nereid; 23, Unfree; 25, Extra; 26, Hyena.

No. 65

ACROSS – 1, Bottle-tree; 8, Victim; 9, Overcharge; 10, Nought; 11, Garden plot; 12, Ingots; 13, Abed; 15, Mooring; 19, Reading; 21, Iona; 22, String; 25, Henceforth; 27, Gibbet; 28, Jack-rafter; 29, Chorea; 30, Reassessed.

DOWN – 1, Brougham; 2, Theirs; 3, Locker; 4, Tramp; 5, Eventide; 6, Scourged; 7, Light tan; 13, Ago; 14, Era; 16, Outright; 17, Rain-bird; 18, Nightjar; 20, Gathered; 23, Aflame; 24, Writes; 26, Cakes.

No. 66

ACROSS – 1, Princes; 5, Bath; 9, Capability Brown; 10, Farm; 11, Liver; 12, Adze; 15, Charade; 16, Salient; 17, Log-book; 19, Frilled; 21, Call; 22, Beard; 23, Owed; 26, Football matches; 27, Peer; 28, New-spun.

DOWN – 1, Pacific; 2, Imperial gallon; 3, Cubs; 4, Saltire; 5, Batters; 6, Tube; 7, Convent; 8, Good-fellowship; 13, Taboo; 14, All in; 17, Lucifer; 18, Kneeler; 19, Foremen; 20, Dodgson; 24, Able; 25, Stew.

No. 67

ACROSS – 1 and 4, Great Bed of Ware; 8, Oasis; 9, Loitering; 11, Each; 12, Acock; 13, Gear; 16, Electric light; 19, Capital fellow; 20, Dime; 22, Agape; 23, Sten; 26, Cartagena; 27, About; 28, Yes, please; 29, Mates.

DOWN – 1, Geometric; 2, Eastcheap; 3, Test; 4, Bulb catalogue; 5, Fief; 6, Aside; 7, Eiger; 10, Inclined plane; 14, Delta; 15, Slyly; 17, Go without; 18, Take notes; 20, Dicky; 21, Marks; 24, Maul; 25, Maim.

No. 68

ACROSS – 1, Just as well; 9, Ko-ko; 10, Came to pass; 11, Throne; 12, Bustler; 15, Tugboat; 16, Digit; 17, Neck; 18, Silo; 19, Charm; 21, Sing out; 22, Sitwell; 24, Rosier; 27, Interposed; 28, Emus; 29, Ruthlessly.

DOWN – 2, Upas; 3, Theist; 4, Spotted; 5, Elan; 6, Last out; 7, Locomotive; 8, Honest toil; 12, Bond Street; 13, Seconds out; 14, Right; 15, Tiers; 19, Currier; 20, Mistral; 23, Whoops; 25, Stet; 26, Fell.

No. 69

ACROSS – 1, Blockades; 9, Erotica; 10, Breezes; 11, Overlie; 12, Shorthorn; 14, Adam's ale; 15, Troops; 17, Rapallo; 20, Onside; 23, Indicate; 25, Adventure; 26, Bruiser; 27, Donates; 28, Not half; 29, Formalist.

DOWN – 2, Lurcher; 3, Cheerio; 4, Arethusa; 5 and 6, Second honeymoon; 7, Gillian; 8, Make sense; 13, Ravaged; 15, Train-band; 16, Precisian; 18, Love poem; 19, Adjusts; 21, Set sail; 22, Darters; 24, Tariff.

No. 70

ACROSS – 1, Vicarage; 5, Cortes; 9, Kangaroo; 10, Hearse; 11, Nineteen; 13, Chased; 14, Rum; 16, Summer; 19, Netball; 20, Crimes; 21, Fry; 26, Treads; 27, Sea-horse; 28, Inured; 29, Slippers; 30, Greasy; 31, Swindler.

DOWN – 1, Viking; 2, Caning; 3, Realty; 4, Glower; 6, Overhaul; 7, Tiresome; 8, Spenders; 12, Numbers; 15, Yes; 16, Sly; 17, Scathing; 18, Sinecure; 19, Needless; 22, Yellow; 23, Chopin; 24, Ordeal; 25, Lessor.

No. 71

ACROSS – 8, Glaucoma; 9, Iberia; 10, Cos; 11, Well-read; 12, Toeing; 13, Centre of gravity; 15, Watches; 18, Stories; 21, Conscience money; 24, Gemini; 25, Up-ending; 26, Ale; 27, Alegar; 28, Succinct.

DOWN – 1, Allege; 2, Pullet; 3, Sole beneficiary; 4, Macduff; 5, Disturb the peace; 6, Receiver; 7, Vignette; 14, Not; 16, Above all; 17, Castings; 19, Ion; 20, Inquest; 22, Ordain; 23, Eunice.

No. 72

ACROSS – 1, Stanhope; 5, Tip-off; 9, Corridor; 10, Askari; 11, Downhill; 12, Smalls; 14, Pin-pointed; 18, Like a leech; 22, Nelson; 23, Pay court; 24, Iberis; 25, Bluebell; 26, Gashes; 27, Islesman.

DOWN – 1, Secede; 2, Arrows; 3, Height; 4, Proclaimed; 6, Insomnia; 7, On a plate; 8, Flip-side; 13, Spectacles; 15, Clanking; 16, Skillets; 17, Caroline; 19, Accede; 20, Museum; 21, Stalin.

No. 73

ACROSS – 1, Excited; 5, Ta-ta; 9, Come in like a lion; 10, Plot; 11, Stood; 12, Veto; 15, Stilled; 16, Forlorn; 17, Without; 19, Bondage; 21, Card; 22, Digit; 23, Cure; 26, List to starboard; 27, Fray; 28, Delayed.

DOWN – 1, Escapes; 2, Common interest; 3, Trip; 4, Deleted; 5, Take-off; 6, Trap; 7, Run down; 8, Wide vocabulary; 13, Allot; 14, Trunk; 17, Wicklow; 18, Thirsty; 19, Brigand; 20, Emended; 24, Stir; 25, Abel.

No. 74

ACROSS – 5, Signal; 8, Clear out; 9, Rosalie; 10, Maple; 11, Straining; 13, Initiate; 14, Limits; 17, Ibo; 19, Pen; 20, Mortal; 23, Compound; 26, Wallpaper; 28, Cases; 29, Billmen; 30, Bowl over; 31, Papers.

DOWN – 1, Scampi; 2, Despair; 3, Artemisia; 4, Purist; 5, Storable; 6, Grain; 7, Alienate; 12, Ten; 15, In a pickle; 16, Mona Lisa; 18, Bloaters; 21, Ace; 22, Cursive; 24, Orator; 25, Desert; 27, Lille.

No. 75

ACROSS – 1, Pickle; 4, Crater; 10, Spanner; 11, Impress; 12, Own; 13, Erith; 14, Rhône; 15, Statisticians; 18, Contact lenses; 23, Upper; 25, Lapse; 26, Ova; 27, Best man; 28, New Year; 29, Duress; 30, Wrists.

Down – 1, Poster; 2, Chariot; 3, Lunch; 5, Roper; 6, Tie down; 7, Rushes; 8, Cross-sections; 9, Windmill-plant; 16, Ain; 17, Ass; 19, Opposer; 20, Express; 21, Curbed; 22, Hearts; 24, Remus; 25, Lower.

No. 76

ACROSS – 1, Chiropodist; 9, Arch; 10, Safety-match; 11, Opal; 14, Maintop; 16, Reposes; 17, David; 18, Nash; 19, Atop; 20, Lever; 22, Ignited; 23, Rat-hole; 24, Lilt; 28, Stockholder; 29, Done; 30, Bearer bonds.

DOWN – 2, Heal; 3, Reel; 4, Plywood; 5, Drab; 6, Seceded; 7, Proposition; 8, Philosopher; 12, Amontillado; 13, Missing link; 15, Paled; 16, River; 20, Legatee; 21, Rancher; 25, Scar; 26, Also; 27, Wend.

No. 77

ACROSS – 1 and 4, Clear the ground; 8, Sidon; 9, Ambitious; 11, Mark; 12, Essay; 13, Otto; 16, Not to be beaten; 19, Sleight-of-hand; 20, Hood; 22, Yacht; 23, Byng; 26, Beefsteak; 27, Agent; 28, Teamsters; 29, Baker.

DOWN – 1, Casemates; 2, Endurance; 3, Ring; 4, Transport café; 5, Rate; 6, U-boat; 7, Disco; 10, Brace of shakes; 14, Stage; 15, Behan; 17, Today week; 18, Navigator; 20, Habit; 21, Opera; 24, Isis; 25, Lamb.

No. 78

ACROSS – 1, Extract; 5, Stand-by; 9, Earthly paradise; 10, Iowa; 11, Denim; 12, Glad; 15, Sent off; 16, Stained; 17, Acheron; 19, Phaeton; 21, Cuts; 22, Odeon; 23, Guam; 26, Down in the depths; 27, Allseed; 28, Returns.

DOWN – 1, Enemies; 2, Threw in the towel; 3, Ashy; 4, Thyself; 5, Sea-pies; 6, Ahab; 7, Drill instructor; 8, Yielded; 13, Loire; 14, Tamar; 17, Arcadia; 18, Nodated; 19, Pioneer; 20, Nemesis; 24, Wife; 25, Meet.

No. 79

ACROSS – 1, Outer space; 9, Plan; 10, Bad weather; 11, Apical; 12, Put down; 15, Rebukes; 16, Lowed; 17, See 3 down; 18, Rind; 19, Snail; 21, Spirits; 22, Topless; 24, Timber; 27, Cover point; 28, Fast; 29, Yellow-spot.

DOWN – 2, Upas; 3 and 17 across, Edward Lear; 4, Sea-fowl; 5, Ache; 6, Enraged; 7, Flick-knife; 8, On all sides; 12, Pulls it off; 13, Tragic muse; 14, Norns; 15, Resit; 19, Starchy; 20, Locarno; 23, Lemons; 25, Oval; 26, Undo.

No. 80

ACROSS – 1, Sinking-funds; 9, Up-ended; 10, Leister; 11, Diva; 12, Madam; 13, Jack; 16, Endives; 17, Tighten; 18, Wagoner; 21, Private; 23, Item; 24, Quart; 25, Jeer; 28, Huddled; 29, Narrate; 30, Intemperance.

DOWN – 1, Shelved; 2, Node; 3, Indians; 4, Gallant; 5, Unit; 6, Detract; 7, Hundredweight; 8, Broken-hearted; 14, Event; 15, Again; 19, Guerdon; 20, Round up; 21, Partner; 22, Average; 26, Flee; 27, Oran.

QUIZZES, GAMES AND PUZZLES

The Book Quiz Book Joseph Connolly

Who was literature's performing flea . . .? Who wrote 'Live Now, Pay Later . . .'? Keats and Cartland, Balzac and Braine, Coleridge conundrums, Eliot enigmas, Tolstoy teasers . . . all in this brilliant quiz book.

The Ultimate Trivia Game Book Maureen and Alan Hiron

If you are immersed in trivia, addicted to quiz games, endlessly nosey, then this is the book for you: over 10,000 pieces of utterly dispensable information!

The Penguin Book of Acrostic Puzzles Albie Fiore

A book of crosswords and a book of quotations in one! Solve the clues provided, fit the letters into the grid provided and make a quotation. It's the most fun you can have with a pen and paper.

Plus five trivia quiz books:
The Royalty Game
The TV Game
The Travel Game
The Pop Game
The Business Game

Crossword Books to baffle and bewilder

Eleven Penguin Books of the *Sun* Crosswords
Eight Penguin books of the *Sunday Times* Crosswords
Seven Penguin Books of *The Times* Crosswords
and Four Jumbo Books of the *Sun* Crosswords
The First Penguin Book of *Daily Express* Crosswords
The Second Penguin Book of *Daily Express* Crosswords

Penguin Crossword Books – something for everyone, however much or little time you have on your hands.